# THE CALM WITHIN

## Releasing Trauma, Anxiety, Stress, and Fear using Natural Therapies

EMBRACING SERENITY THROUGH ESSENTIAL OILS, SPIRITUAL RESPONSE THERAPY, BIOMAGNETIC PAIR THERAPY, NATURAL SUPPLEMENTS, MEDITATION, HYPNOTHERAPY

**BROOKS ALLISEN M.H. C.Ht.**

The Calm Within: Releasing Trauma, Anxiety, Stress, and Fear Using Natural Therapies

Embracing Serenity through Essential Oils, Spiritual Response Therapy, Biomagnetic Pair Therapy, Natural Supplements, Meditation, Hypnotherapy



Disclaimer

In "The Calm Within," the author emphasizes the significance of privacy and sensitivity surrounding case studies. These examples spotlight the transformative potential of Essential Oils, Spiritual Response Therapy, Biomagnetic Pair Therapy, Natural Supplements, Meditation, and Hypnotherapy in alleviating trauma, anxiety, stress, and fear.

# THE CALM WITHIN

To honor clients' privacy, all names, identities, and locations have been altered. This ethical approach safeguards their personal experiences' confidentiality while upholding the authenticity of their healing journeys.

The case studies in "The Calm Within" illustrate the power of natural therapies for emotional well-being, inspiring readers through firsthand stories of serenity found amidst emotional challenges.

This book offers insights into natural therapies' potential, such as Essential Oils, Spiritual Response Therapy, Biomagnetic Pair Therapy, Natural Supplements, Meditation, and Hypnotherapy, to address emotional distress. It's crucial to note that the content isn't intended for medical diagnosis, treatment, or remedies.

The author, publisher, and contributors disclaim any liability for outcomes arising from the information's use or misuse. This content provides general guidance and should not replace professional medical advice. Consult a healthcare provider for personalized medical concerns.

Within "The Calm Within," you'll witness the power of hope, resilience, and growth. These case studies exemplify the  mpact of natural therapies on emotional well-being, offering a glimpse into the profound serenity that awaits.

In order to create a more reader-friendly experience, the author has employed computer-assisted tools throughout the process of assembling, writing, and organizing the content of this book. The author has closely supervised and examined the information produced by these tools to ensure its accuracy and comprehensiveness. Additionally, computer-generated or digitally enhanced images have been included in this book to enrich the reader's educational journey and showcase the potential of natural therapies in alleviating trauma, anxiety, stress, and fears.

# Contents

*Dedication:*

*To the unwavering pillars of support,*

*For those who battle their own storms within,*

*To the compassionate professionals who light the way,*

*And to the caring souls, near and far, who embrace with love.*

*This book is dedicated to you all,*

*The guiding stars in the darkest of nights,*

*Your empathy, strength, and boundless love,*

*Illuminate the path to healing and hope.*

*In the face of traumas, anxieties, stress, and fears,*

*You stand strong, lifting the burden with grace,*

*To family, friends, caregivers, and neighbors,*

*Thank you for your unwavering embrace.*

*Together, we navigate life's tumultuous seas,*

*With your kindness, we find the calm within,*

*This dedication is a humble tribute,*

*To the heroes of empathy and resilience.*

# About the Author

"Words are a lens to focus one's mind.'

- Ayn Rand

## **Brooks Allisen, M.H. C.Ht.**

I've had a variety of special interests in healing for the past 30 years or so. It started when our daughter simultaneously suffered a bout of Mononucleosis, Coxsackie, and Epstein Bars Viruses that seriously jeopardized her health. Her family doctor wanted to put her on steroids to basically knock out her immune system. That didn't feel right, so we found a naturalistic medical doctor who understood the immune system. He recommended a protocol of vitamins, minerals, amino acids, and essential fatty acids, and within a few days, our daughter had recovered 85% of her health. That episode opened our eyes to looking more holistically at our health.

When we moved to Vancouver Island, we met many people who had the same health interests. We became vegetarian and were supported by others in a veggie pot-luck group. We found alternative healing practitioners who enlightened us on many subjects that we had little experience with, such as healing with crystals and energy fields. They introduced us to many modes of therapies that enable us to connect our inner energies so we experience harmony within ourselves and with others.

As we progressed, we learned various techniques of natural therapeutic healing methods, including Healing Touch,

Therapeutic Touch, Spiritual Response Therapy, Spiritual Restructuring, Rieke, Hypnotherapy, Biomagnetic Pair Therapy, and others.

Since 2000, I've been a passionate practitioner in the field of Spiritual Response Therapy (SRT) and Spiritual Restructuring (SpR). SRT helps clients remove energetic blocks stemming from past lives and memories. These blocks often manifest as obstacles in various aspects of life, such as hampering prosperity and personal growth.

I am also a Biomagnetic Pair Therapy practitioner. Biomagnetic Pair Therapy provides clients with the opportunity to experience healing by way of balancing magnetic and electrical signals at the cellular level.

From 1997 onward, I've had a special interest in essential oils and have created several unique blends which many people have found to be very effective.

I am dedicated to empowering my clients on their journey towards healing, self-awareness, and success.

This book provides a transformative journey for readers to find ways to break free from the limitations that may have been holding them back, to help unlock the limitless possibilities of one's true self.

If you're prepared to embark on a life-changing journey and break free from the limitations that might be holding you back, I extend an invitation to explore the pages of The Calm

Within. You can delve deeper into the incredible power of Natural Therapies to take the first step toward transformation and discover the possibilities that await you.

### *"Shining Through"*

*In life's vast sea, through storms we steer,*
*Adversity's waves, we'll persevere.*
*The darkest night, a canvas anew,*
*Our light shines bright, strong, and true.*

# Preface

## Exploring Natural Therapies: A World Beyond Conventional Medicine

In the journey towards well-being and healing, one often encounters a rich tapestry of terms, each weaving a unique perspective on the path to health and serenity. "The Calm Within" not only delves into natural therapies but also invites readers to explore the diverse world of holistic healing. Here, we shine a light on some common names, terms, and categories often used interchangeably with "natural therapies."

1. Complementary and Alternative Medicine (CAM): This umbrella term encompasses a wide array of therapies and practices that exist alongside or in conjunction with conventional medicine. CAM includes herbal remedies, acupuncture, meditation, and more, focusing on treating the whole person, not just the symptoms.
2. Holistic Healing: Holistic healing takes a comprehensive approach to well-being, addressing not only physical symptoms but also considering mental, emotional, and

spiritual aspects. It emphasizes the interconnectedness of these facets in achieving balance and health.

3. Traditional Medicine: Rooted in cultural practices and indigenous knowledge, traditional medicine has been passed down through generations. It often involves herbal remedies, rituals, and spiritual healing techniques that have stood the test of time.

4. Home Remedies: These are simple, everyday solutions to common health issues, often using ingredients found in one's home or natural surroundings. From honey for a sore throat to aloe vera for skin ailments, home remedies are a testament to nature's healing power.

5. Herbal Remedies: Herbal remedies involve the use of plants and plant extracts for medicinal purposes. Plants like lavender, chamomile, and ginger have been valued for their healing properties for centuries.

6. Integrative Medicine: This approach blends conventional medicine with alternative therapies to address the whole person. It aims to provide the most effective and evidence-based treatments while considering individual preferences and needs.

7. Mind-Body Therapies: These practices, such as yoga and tai chi, recognize the connection between mental and physical health. By fostering mindfulness and relaxation, they promote holistic well-being.

8. Energy Healing: Energy healing therapies, like Reiki and biofield therapies, work on the premise that the body has an energy field that can be balanced and restored to pro-

mote health. These therapies tap into the body's innate healing abilities.

9. Alternative Treatments: Often seen as alternatives to conventional medical approaches, these treatments include acupuncture, chiropractic care, and naturopathy. They offer unique perspectives on healing and wellness.

10. Non-Conventional Medicine: This term encompasses any approach to healing that falls outside the realm of conventional, Western medicine. It highlights the diversity of options available to individuals seeking alternative paths to health.

As "The Calm Within" beautifully illustrates, natural therapies and these related terms offer a vast landscape of healing possibilities. What's most important is finding the approach that resonates with your individual needs and preferences. Whether you explore herbal remedies, embrace energy healing, or integrate holistic practices into your life, the journey to well-being is a personal one, and it's about discovering the serenity that lies within.

The techniques and therapies available in The Calm Within can be beneficial for individuals of all ages, ranging from children and teenagers to adults and seniors. These natural therapies encompass everyone, aiming to bring about a sense of tranquility, peace, and healing.

*Savor the Calm in Simple Living.*

# Introduction

Welcome to *The Calm Within*, a transformative journey towards healing the mind, nurturing the soul, and experiencing the profound wonders of inner peace and harmony. In this book, we will delve into the realms of Essential Oils, Spiritual Response Therapy, Biomagnetic Pair Therapy, Meditation, Hypnotherapy, Universal Energy, and more, uncovering their remarkable potential to bring tranquility and balance to our lives.

## Chapter 1: Essential Oils - Nature's Gift for Healing and Emotional Well-being

First, we will explore the world of essential oils, which are nature's gift for healing and emotional well-being. Essential oils are highly concentrated plant extracts that capture the pure essence of aromatic plants. Essential oils have been used for centuries to help with physical, emotional, and spiritual health. Learn how essential oils interact with the body and affect emotions, along with their ability to ease and desensitize negative emotions and feelings associated with trauma, anxiety, stress, and fear.

## Chapter 2: Spiritual Response Therapy Removes Psychological Programs

Find out how Spiritual Response Therapy (SRT) frees us from the shackles of past traumas and negative belief systems. Through this modality, we can release emotional blockages, dissolve patterns of self-sabotage, and embrace a life of freedom and authenticity.

## Chapter 3: Biomagnetic Pair Therapy Helps Resolve Emotional Blocks/Issues

Uncover the revolutionary Biomagnetic Pair Therapy (BMP), which restores electromagnetic balance and creates an environment that inhibits restores function and pathogens that disrupt our energetic well-being. By harmonizing the body's magnetic fields, BMP helps us regain emotional equilibrium, fostering a sense of peace and harmony within.

## Chapter 4: Natural Supplements Build Healthy Neurological Pathways

Explore the world of natural supplements and their ability to support and enhance our neurological health. From mood-regulating herbs to brain-boosting nutrients, we uncover some of the secrets of building resilient neural pathways, promoting mental clarity, and nurturing overall cognitive well-being.

## Chapter 5: Meditation and Relaxation Therapy Calms Nerves and Restores Focus

Embark on a journey of stillness and inner tranquility through meditation and relaxation therapy. Learn various techniques that calm the nerves, reduce stress, and restore focus, enabling us to navigate life's challenges with grace and clarity.

## Chapter 6: Hypnotherapy Clears Unhealthy Emotions and Resets Feelings of Happiness

Discover the profound potential of hypnotherapy in unlocking the subconscious mind, clearing unhealthy emotions, and resetting our feelings of happiness. By accessing the hidden depths of our psyche, we can reprogram self-limiting beliefs and cultivate a positive and joyful outlook on life.

## Chapter 7: Universal Energy - Tap into the Healing Power of the Universe

In this enlightening chapter, we explore the transformative nature of universal energy and its ability to bring harmony and balance to our being. By harnessing the energetic forces that permeate the universe, we restore our inner vitality, align with our true essence, and experience profound healing at a soul level.

Universal energy, also known as life force energy or chi, flows through all living things and connects us to the divine source of existence. By understanding and working with this subtle yet potent energy, we access a limitless wellspring of healing and spiritual growth.

## Chapter 8: Tips, Hints, and Techniques for Building Inner Harmony

As an added bonus, we have included a chapter filled with practical tips, hints, and techniques to help overcome anxiety and reduce negative feelings. From stress management strategies to self-care rituals, this chapter offers invaluable insights to support your journey toward lasting calm and inner harmony.

## Introduction Summary

Throughout this book, you will discover various techniques and practices to harness the power of Essential Oils, Spiritual Response Therapy, Biomagnetic Pair Therapy, Meditation, Hypnotherapy, and Universal Energy. These modalities guide you on a path of self-empowerment and holistic healing, enabling you to find inner peace, conquer trauma, anxiety, stress, and fear, and nurture your soul.

By incorporating the wonders of Essential Oils, Spiritual Response Therapy, Biomagnetic Pair Therapy, Meditation, Hypnotherapy, and Universal Energy, into your life, you embark on a path of self-empowerment and holistic healing. May this book serve as a trusted companion, inspiring and guiding you toward a state of calm, where the mind is healed, the soul is nurtured, and inner peace becomes your truest essence.

Take a deep breath, open your heart, and start on your journey of self-discovery and inner transformation. In The Calm Within, read about the wonders of Essential Oils, Spiritual Response Therapy, Biomagnetic Pair Therapy, Meditation, Hypnotherapy, and Universal Energy, to get ready for your quest for inner harmony and well-being.

May this book serve as a trusted companion, inspiring and guiding you toward a state of calm, where the mind is healed, the soul is nurtured, and inner peace becomes your truest essence.

The transformative powers of The Calm Within await you.

*Rise above. Find your calm.*

*Let the countryside heal your spirit.*

# Essential Oils Ease and Desensitize Negative Emotions and Feelings

"Although the world is full of suffering, it is also full of the overcoming of it."

– Helen Keller

*Essential oils: your path to tranquility.*

## Understanding the Science Behind Essential Oils: How They Interact with the Body and Affect Emotions.

In the journey of healing the mind and nurturing the soul, understanding the science behind essential oils is an essential stepping stone. These remarkable plant extracts possess unique properties that interact with the body and influence emotions in profound ways. By exploring the world of essential oils, you can discover the science behind their therapeutic effects and how they can affect your emotional conditions.

Essential oils are concentrated extracts derived from various parts of plants, including leaves, flowers, bark, and roots. They capture the plant's aromatic compounds, which are responsible for their distinct fragrances and therapeutic qualities. When inhaled or applied to the skin, these potent compounds engage with the body through several mechanisms.

One primary method is through olfaction, the sense of smell. The aroma of essential oils triggers the olfactory system, directly affecting the limbic system in the brain. The limbic system is directly related to our emotions, memory, and hormonal regulation. As essential oil molecules are inhaled, they reach the olfactory receptors, sending signals to the brain and eliciting emotional responses.

Furthermore, essential oils can be absorbed through the skin. When applied to the skin, they penetrate the skin, to enter the bloodstream, allowing their components to circulate throughout the body. As they travel, essential oils interact with neurotransmitters, hormones, and other biochemical messengers, influencing emotional states and promoting relaxation.

Each essential oil possesses a unique chemical composition, contributing to its specific therapeutic properties. For instance, lavender oil contains linalool and linalyl acetate, which exhibit calming and soothing effects. Otherwise, citrus oils like bergamot and sweet orange contain limonene, known for their uplifting and energizing benefits. Understanding these chemical constituents helps in selecting the most appropriate essential oils for targeted emotional support.

It is important to note that essential oils work holistically, addressing both the physical and emotional aspects of well-being. By nurturing the mind, they simultaneously nurture the soul. Incorporating essential oils into your daily routine can provide a powerful tool for emotional self-care and promote a sense of inner harmony.

As you continue your exploration of essential oils, remember to embrace their wonders with curiosity and an open heart. Together, let us uncover the transformative potential of these natural remedies, as we embark on a journey towards conquering trauma, anxiety, stress, and fear naturally.

## Identifying the Most Effective Essential Oils for Calming Anxiety and Reducing Stress

In the quest for healing the mind and nurturing the soul, essential oils offer a natural and powerful ally in calming anxiety and reducing stress. These incredible plant extracts have been cherished for centuries for their soothing properties and ability to promote a sense of tranquility. In this section, we will explore the most effective essential oils for finding peace amidst the chaos of daily life.

Lavender, renowned for its calming aroma, takes the spotlight as one of the most effective essential oils for anxiety and stress relief. Its gentle, floral scent has a profound impact on the nervous system, promoting relaxation and restful sleep. Lavender essential oil can be diffused in the air, applied topically to pulse points, diffused, or added to bathwater for a calming and rejuvenating experience.

Another gem in the realm of relaxation is chamomile essential oil. Its gentle, apple-like fragrance possesses remarkable properties that help ease anxiety and soothe frayed nerves. Often used in aromatherapy, chamomile essential oil can be diffused or added to massage oils for a blissful and tranquil experience.

Citrus oils, such as bergamot and sweet orange, offer an uplifting and refreshing solution to combat stress and anxiety. Bursting with bright, citrusy aromas, these oils have a mood-boosting effect that can help uplift the spirits and promote a positive outlook. Diffusing these oils or adding a few drops to a warm bath can create a cheerful and invigorating atmosphere.

For those seeking a grounding and calming influence, vetiver essential oil is an excellent choice. With its earthy and woody aroma, vetiver helps instill a sense of stability and emotional balance. By grounding and centering the mind, vetiver essential oil can alleviate anxiety and provide a soothing effect. Consider using it in a diffuser or diluting it in a carrier oil for a relaxing massage.

Finally, the enchanting scent of ylang-ylang essential oil holds remarkable potential for easing stress and promoting inner peace. Its exotic and floral fragrance has a harmonizing effect on the mind and emotions. Incorporating ylang-ylang essential oil into your self-care routine through diffusing or applying it topically can help release tension and encourage a sense of calm.

Remember, everyone's response to essential oils may vary, so it is essential to find the oils that resonate with you personally. Experimentation and self-discovery are key in identifying the most effective essential oils for your unique needs.

By incorporating these precious botanical extracts into your daily routine, you can harness their incredible power to calm anxiety and reduce stress. Allow the soothing scents of lavender, chamomile, citrus oils, vetiver, and ylang-ylang to bathe you in an aroma of tranquility, as you begin your transformative journey towards inner harmony.

## Developing Self-Care Rituals: Incorporating Essential Oils into Daily Routines for Emotional Balance

In the pursuit of healing the mind and nurturing the soul, establishing self-care rituals is paramount. These intentional practices offer moments of respite and restoration in our fast-paced lives. Essential oils, with their remarkable therapeutic properties, can play a transformative role in enhancing our emotional well-being. In this part, we explore the art of developing self-care rituals that incorporate essential oils into your daily routines, fostering a sense of balance and harmony.

## Morning Rituals:

Start your day with an invigorating boost by incorporating essential oils into your morning routine. Add a few drops of citrus essential oils like lemon, grapefruit, or orange to your shower gel or body lotion for an uplifting and energizing experience. The vibrant scents will awaken your senses, leaving you feeling refreshed and ready to tackle the day ahead.

## Mid-Day Retreats:

During the hustle and bustle of the day, taking a moment to pause and recharge can make a significant difference. Create a mini-retreat by keeping a roll-on bottle of your favorite essential oil blend in your bag or desk drawer. Whenever stress or anxiety starts to creep in, simply apply a swipe to your pulse points, temples, or the back of your neck. Breathe deeply, allowing the aroma to envelop you, and feel the tension melt away.

## Evening Wind-Down:

As the day draws to a close, it's essential to create a tranquil atmosphere that promotes relaxation and prepares you for a restful night's sleep. Consider diffusing calming essential oils such as lavender, chamomile, or ylang-ylang in your bedroom before bedtime. The gentle fragrance will soothe your senses and create a peaceful ambiance, setting the stage for a night of deep rejuvenation.

## Mindful Moments:

Incorporating essential oils into mindfulness practices can deepen your connection with the present moment. Before meditation, yoga, or deep breathing exercises, apply a few drops of grounding oils like sandalwood or vetiver to the palms of your hands. Cup your hands over your nose, take slow, deep breaths, and let the aroma guide you into a state of tranquility and focus.

## Transition Rituals:

Transitions can be challenging, whether it's moving from work to personal time or from a busy day to a restful evening. Essential oils can help create a smooth shift by signaling to your mind and body that it's time to unwind. Develop a transition ritual that involves diffusing comforting oils like cedarwood or frankincense, allowing the aroma to envelop your space and facilitate the transition from one state to another.

By integrating essential oils into your self-care rituals, you infuse everyday moments with intention, allowing their therapeutic properties to support emotional balance and well-being. Whether you choose to incorporate them into your morning routine, mid-day retreats, evening wind-down, mindful moments, or transition rituals, these aromatic companions will enhance your journey toward inner harmony.

Remember, self-care is a personal and ever-evolving practice. Allow yourself the freedom to experiment, explore, and discover the rituals that resonate most deeply with you. Embrace the wonders of essential oils as you embark on a path of self-care, nurturing both your mind and soul.

## Dealing with Trauma Triggers: Harnessing Essential Oils to Support Emotional Healing and Manage Triggers

In the process of healing the mind and nurturing the soul, it is essential to address the effects of trauma triggers on our emotional well-being. Traumatic experiences can leave deep imprints, and certain triggers can evoke overwhelming emotions and stress responses. Following, we explore the power of essential oils in supporting emotional healing and managing trauma triggers, offering a path towards resilience and inner peace.

Essential oils provide a natural and gentle approach to navigating the complexities of trauma triggers. Their aromatic compounds can influence the limbic system, the emotional center of the brain, and help restore a sense of balance and calm. Here are some ways to harness their therapeutic benefits:

Calming Essential Oils: Lavender, known for its soothing properties, can be incredibly helpful in managing trauma triggers. Its gentle scent can promote relaxation and alleviate anxiety. Applying a diluted lavender oil blend to pulse points or using a lavender-infused room spray during triggering moments can provide a grounding and calming effect.

Uplifting Essential Oils: Citrus oils, such as bergamot or grapefruit, possess refreshing and uplifting qualities that can help shift your emotional state during triggering situations. Diffusing these oils or using them in a personal inhaler can promote a sense of positivity and resilience.

Grounding Essential Oils: Vetiver and frankincense essential oils offer grounding and stabilizing properties that can support emotional healing. Applying a diluted blend of these oils to the soles of your feet or inhaling their aroma can help anchor you in the present moment and provide a sense of stability.

Comforting Essential Oils: Chamomile and rose essential oils are known for their nurturing and comforting qualities. When triggers arise, creating a soothing atmosphere with these oils can offer solace and emotional support. Consider diffusing these oils or using them in a warm bath to create a safe space for healing.

Personalized Blends: Each individual's experience with trauma triggers is unique, and finding the right essential oil blend may require experimentation. Working with a qualified aromatherapist or exploring different blends that resonate with your personal needs can help you discover the most effective combination for managing your triggers.

Remember, essential oils are one tool in a comprehensive approach to healing trauma triggers. It is important to seek support from mental health professionals and engage in other therapeutic modalities to address the root causes of trauma and promote overall well-being.

By incorporating essential oils into your healing journey, you can create a supportive and nurturing environment to manage trauma triggers. Embrace the wonders of these natural remedies as you navigate the path toward emotional healing, resilience, and inner harmony.

## Enhancing Sleep and Reducing Insomnia: Using Essential Oils to Promote Relaxation and Improve Sleep Quality

A restful night's sleep is vital for healing the mind and nurturing the soul. Yet, in our fast-paced and stressful world, many individuals struggle with insomnia and sleep disturbances. If you find yourself tossing and turning, trying to get some sleep, these essential oils may help. In this section of this chapter, we delve into the art of using essential oils to promote relaxation and enhance sleep quality, offering you a path to rejuvenation and inner harmony.

Lavender Essential Oil: Lavender reigns as one of the most effective essential oils for sleep. Its calming and soothing aroma helps reduce anxiety and encourages a restful state. Diffusing lavender essential oil in your bedroom or using a lavender-infused pillow spray can create a tranquil sleep environment.

*Lavender love for inner calm.*

Roman Chamomile Essential Oil: With its gentle and comforting scent, Roman chamomile essential oil has long been valued for its ability to promote relaxation. Diffusing this oil or adding a few drops to a warm bath before bedtime can help ease tension and prepare your mind and body for a peaceful night's sleep.

Sweet Marjoram Essential Oil: Sweet marjoram essential oil has sedative properties, making it a great help for those having trouble sleeping. This oil can be diffused, diluted in a carrier oil for a relaxing massage, or added to a warm compress to calm the nervous system and promote deep, restorative sleep.

Vetiver Essential Oil: Vetiver essential oil offers a grounding and earthy aroma that can help quiet an overactive mind and promote relaxation. Diffusing vetiver oil in the evening or creating a bedtime ritual with a vetiver-infused body lotion can aid in easing anxiety and preparing the body for restful sleep.

Bergamot Essential Oil: Bergamot essential oil, with its citrusy and uplifting scent, has mood-balancing properties that can help alleviate stress and anxiety before bedtime. Diffusing bergamot oil or adding a few drops to a warm bath can create a soothing environment and promote a sense of calm.

It's important to remember that everyone's response to essential oils may vary. Experimentation and finding the oils that resonate with you personally are key to enhancing your sleep. Additionally, practicing good sleep hygiene, such as creating a peaceful sleep environment, establishing a regular bedtime routine, and avoiding stimulating activities before bed, can further support the effectiveness of essential oils.

Incorporating essential oils into your nighttime routine is a gentle and natural approach to enhancing sleep and reducing insomnia. The aroma of lavender, Roman chamomile, sweet marjoram, vetiver, and bergamot improves sleep quality and overall better health.

## Building Resilience and Emotional Strength: How Essential Oils Can Support the Process of Overcoming Adversity and Building Emotional Resilience

Life is full of challenges and adversities that can test our emotional strength. Building resilience is crucial for navigating these difficult times and emerging stronger on the other side. Here, we explore the transformative power of essential oils in supporting the process of overcoming adversity and building emotional resilience, offering you a path to inner strength and harmony.

Frankincense Essential Oil: Frankincense has been revered for centuries for its grounding and centering properties. Its rich aroma can help foster emotional stability and promote a sense of inner strength. Diffusing frankincense oil during times of stress or uncertainty can provide a comforting and supportive atmosphere.

*Roses: Nature's gift to soothe the soul.*

Rose Essential Oil: Known as the "queen of essential oils," rose oil offers a beautiful and uplifting scent that can help cultivate feelings of love, compassion, and resilience. Incorporating rose essential oil into your self-care rituals, such as using it in a relaxing bath or applying it as a perfume, can inspire a sense of emotional strength and self-nurturing.

Cedarwood Essential Oil: Cedarwood essential oil has a warm and woody aroma that can instill feelings of confidence and stability. It can help create a sense of grounding during challenging times. Diffusing cedarwood oil or blending it with a carrier oil for a calming massage can support emotional resilience.

Bergamot Essential Oil: Bergamot essential oil possesses uplifting and mood-balancing properties. Its citrusy aroma can help alleviate feelings of anxiety and promote a positive mindset. Diffusing bergamot oil or adding a few drops to a personal inhaler can provide a boost of emotional strength and resilience.

Ylang-Ylang Essential Oil: Ylang-ylang essential oil offers a sweet and floral scent that promotes relaxation and helps release tension. This oil can aid in the process of letting go of negative emotions and embracing a more resilient mindset. Adding ylang-ylang oil to your self-care routine, such as using it in a diffuser or incorporating it into a massage blend, can support emotional healing and strength.

Remember, essential oils are not a magical solution on their own, but they can be powerful allies in your journey toward emotional resilience. Combine their use with self-reflection, self-care practices, and seeking support from trusted professionals when needed.

As you overcome adversity and build emotional resilience, embrace the wonders of frankincense, rose, cedarwood, bergamot, and ylang-ylang essential oils. Allow their transformative properties to support your inner strength and guide you toward a place of resilience, healing, and profound personal growth.

## Summary of Chapter 1:

In this chapter of The Calm Within, you have embarked on a journey towards conquering trauma, anxiety, stress, and fear naturally through the exploration of essential oils, and you have gained a deep understanding of these modalities and their profound impact on your inner harmony and emotional well-being. The key insights from each of the above aspects of essential oils provide you with a comprehensive overview of the transformative power of essential oils in helping you conquer trauma, anxiety, stress, and fear naturally.

1 - Understanding the Science Behind Essential Oils: How They Interact with the Body and Affect Emotions - Uncovering the fascinating science behind essential oils, including their molecular composition and interaction with our senses. Learning how essential oils can influence emotions, promote relaxation, and restore balance in the mind and body.

2 - Identifying the Most Effective Essential Oils for Calming Anxiety and Reducing Stress: Discovering the soothing properties of essential oils such as lavender, chamomile, and bergamot. These oils used daily may reduce anxiety, reduce stress, and may promote emotional well-being.

3 - Developing Self-Care Rituals: Incorporating Essential Oils into Daily Routines for Emotional Balance: Learning the art of self-care rituals and how essential oils can enhance your well-being. Exploring the power of aromatherapy, massage, and personal care products infused with essential oils to cre-

ate moments of tranquility, emotional balance, ard self-nurturing.

4 - Dealing with Trauma Triggers: Harnessing Essential Oils to Support Emotional Healing and Manage Triggers: Uncovering the role of essential oils in managing trauma triggers and supporting emotional healing. Exploring the transformative potential of oils such as frankincense, rose, and vetiver in creating a safe and nurturing environment for emotional growth and resilience.

5 - Enhancing Sleep and Reducing Insomnia: Using Essential Oils to Promote Relaxation and Improve Sleep Quality: Delving into the world of essential oils for sleep enhancement and insomnia relief. Discover the calming properties of oils like lavender, cedarwood, and ylang-ylang, and learn how to create a peaceful bedtime routine that promotes deep relaxation and restful sleep.

6 - Building Resilience and Emotional Strength: How Essential Oils Can Support the Process of Overcoming Adversity and Building Emotional Resilience: Exploring the use of essential oils in building emotional resilience and overcoming adversity. Discovering oils such as frankincense, rosemary, and lemon can empower you to navigate life's challenges with strength, clarity, and inner balance.

By embracing the wonders of essential oils, along with the other holistic therapies discussed in this book, you have equipped yourself with powerful tools for healing the mind and nurturing the soul. Each aspect of this book provides you with valuable insights and practical guidance on incorporating these modalities into your daily life.

You are unique - your body, your mind, and your psyche. Allow yourself to explore, experiment, and discover the combination of essential oils that resonate with your individual needs.

As you embark on this transformative path towards inner harmony, may the wisdom and practices shared in this book guide you to conquer trauma, anxiety, stress, and fear naturally, and empower you to live a life filled with emotional well-being and profound self-discovery.

### The Sun's First Kiss

*As the sun bestows its morning kiss,*
*Tranquility emerges from the mist.*
*In dawn's embrace, the world's at ease,*
*Serenity dances among the trees.*

# Spiritual Response Therapy Clears Destructive and Limiting Programs

"The soul always knows what to do to heal itself.
The challenge is to silence the mind."

- Caroline Myss

*Unlock the past to find peace in the present*

## Previous Lives Experiences Create Blocks that Limit Our Abilities Today

In the captivating realm of Spiritual Response Therapy (SRT), profound healing awaits those who seek to release the burdens of past traumas and negative belief systems. Through the transformative power of SRT, individuals can embark on a journey towards emotional liberation, reclaiming their true essence and experiencing a newfound sense of inner peace and harmony. Here are ten important effects of SRT that can significantly impact individuals suffering from trauma, anxiety, and fear:

Healing Trauma: SRT provides a safe and effective method to address and heal trauma at its core. It helps individuals release emotional blockages, empowering them to move forward with renewed strength and resilience.

Emotional Liberation: By identifying and clearing negative psychological programs, SRT frees individuals from self-sabotaging patterns, allowing them to break free from the chains of fear, anxiety, and limiting beliefs.

Overcoming Anxiety: SRT offers a pathway to alleviate anxiety by addressing the root causes that contribute to its manifestation. Through the removal of energetic blockages and the clearing of subconscious patterns, individuals can experience a newfound sense of calm and tranquility.

Releasing Fear: SRT assists in the release of deep-rooted fears that may hinder personal growth and well-being. By addressing the origin of fear-based programs, individuals can cultivate courage, resilience, and a greater sense of empowerment.

Restoring Inner Peace: Through the process of clearing psychological programs, SRT helps restore inner peace and harmony. Individuals experience a sense of balance, alignment, and connection to their authentic selves.

Enhancing Emotional Resilience: SRT empowers individuals to build emotional resilience by addressing and clearing past wounds and negative patterns. This newfound resilience enables individuals to navigate life's challenges with greater ease and grace.

Cultivating Self-Awareness: SRT facilitates a deeper understanding of oneself, fostering self-awareness and self-discovery. It allows individuals to explore their subconscious mind, uncover hidden beliefs, and make conscious choices aligned with their true desires.

Releasing Limiting Beliefs: SRT assists in identifying and releasing limiting beliefs that may hinder personal growth and success. By clearing these beliefs, individuals can embrace their full potential and create a life of abundance and fulfillment.

Restoring Trust and Confidence: Through the clearing of destructive and limiting programs, SRT helps individuals rebuild trust in themselves and their ability to navigate life's challenges. It restores confidence, empowering individuals to step into their authentic power.

Cultivating Spiritual Connection: SRT offers a pathway to deepen one's spiritual connection and explore the higher realms of consciousness. Through the clearing of energetic blockages, individuals can access their innate spiritual wisdom and embrace a more profound sense of purpose and meaning.

These ten effects highlight the transformative potential of Spiritual Response Therapy (SRT) in addressing trauma, anxiety, and fear. By embarking on this journey of self-discovery and emotional healing, individuals can experience a profound shift towards inner peace, emotional well-being, and a renewed zest for life.

## Understanding the carrying forward of programs from past lives into the present is a key aspect of Spiritual Response Therapy

Delving into the intricate workings of the soul's journey, Spiritual Response Therapy (SRT) sheds light on how these programs can influence our current experiences and emotions. Discovering the mechanisms behind this process can offer valuable insights into our personal growth and healing.

The carrying forward of programs refers to the transfer of unresolved emotions, traumas, and patterns from previous lifetimes to our current existence. According to Spiritual Response Therapy, the soul accumulates a wealth of experiences and knowledge throughout its various incarnations. While some experiences may have been positive and empowering, others may have left deep imprints of pain, fear, or limiting beliefs.

These imprints, often referred to as programs, can persist across lifetimes and continue to affect us in subtle or profound ways. They can manifest as recurring patterns, self-sabotaging behaviors, unexplained fears, or chronic emotional and physical ailments. Spiritual Response Therapy recognizes that these programs are not limited to a single lifetime but can carry significant influence over our present reality.

The process of how programs are carried forward is believed to involve the soul's energy and its connection to the Akashic Records. The Akashic Records are said to be an ethereal repository of information that holds the records of all souls and their experiences throughout time. It is within these records that the imprints and unresolved issues from past lives reside.

During a Spiritual Response Therapy session, a trained practitioner accesses the Akashic Records through a form of spiritual dowsing or intuitive guidance. The SRT practitioner uses a series of charts and questions to identify and address the programs that are impacting an individual's current life experiences. By connecting with the higher self and spiritual guides, the practitioner assists in releasing and healing these programs, allowing for personal growth, transformation, and the resolution of past-life issues.

The understanding of how programs are carried forward from past lives into the present offers a profound perspective on the interconnectedness of our experiences across time. It highlights the opportunity for healing and personal evolution by addressing the root causes of our challenges and limitations.

In summary, Spiritual Response Therapy recognizes that unresolved programs from past lives can influence our current emotions, behaviors, and well-being. By accessing the Akashic Records and working with spiritual guidance, this therapy aims to release and heal these programs, allowing individuals to transcend the limitations of their past and embrace a more empowered and fulfilling life.

## The Origins, Development, Processes, Practices, and Other Information Regarding Spiritual Response Therapy (SRT) and Spiritual Restructuring (SpR)

Spiritual Response Therapy (SRT) is a remarkable spiritual healing technique that aims to remove blocks hindering individuals from living happier lives. It operates on a spiritual level, addressing spiritual, mental, emotional, and physical challenges to enhance various aspects of life. Developed by Robert E. Detzler in 1988, SRT is a systematic approach to researching the subconscious mind and soul records to identify and release discordant, limiting ideas. These ideas are cleared and are then replaced on a spiritual level, with loving and supportive beliefs, enabling individuals to transform their inner and outer lives and experience greater freedom.

In SRT, practitioners utilize their muscle responses to bypass the conscious mind and negative programming, facilitating communication with the subconscious and the inner guidance within. A pendulum serves as a movement amplifier and pointer, aiding in the interaction with the individual's High Self using specialized charts. Through this process, old programs can be cleared and then replaced on a spiritual level, with positive energy and inner peace, leading to clearer and more joyful lives for thousands of people.

One of the key aspects of Spiritual Response Therapy is clearing past lives and negative energies that hinder individuals from reaching their highest potential. By delving into past life energies, subconscious blocks, and negative soul programming, SRT helps identify and clear these obstacles from the subconscious and soul (Akashic) records. This clearing process enables individuals to heal themselves on all levels, paving the way for personal growth and self-realization.

To learn and practice Spiritual Response Therapy, individuals can participate in SRT Basic and Advanced classes, which are available globally. The SRT Basic class offers expert supervision as participants communicate with their High Self to clear and understand their own Akashic records, subconscious negative programs and beliefs, past life energies, and subconscious blocks. Additionally, the class provides insights into harmonizing relationships, empowering oneself for a higher purpose, and assisting friends and family.

For those who have completed the Basic training class, Advanced classes and Review classes are also available. These subsequent training sessions, conducted by Certified SRT Teachers, allow individuals to deepen their understanding and refine their skills in utilizing SRT for research, clearing negative energies, and addressing blocking memories.

Apart from Spiritual Response Therapy, another related modality is Spiritual Restructuring (SpR). SpR focuses on correcting imbalances in the body to establish greater health. It addresses muscle imbalances, adjusts bones and tissues, and works with organs and glands to restore their proper positions and promote healing. SpR can also release stressful body memories from past lives and resolve energetic programs held within the body.

In SpR classes, individuals learn techniques to physically (energetically, off the body) and spiritually adjust various body parts, release tension in muscles, gain knowledge of nutrition for different bodily systems, harmonize the brain and mind, practice meditation for emotional release, and utilize spiritual energy for organ and gland healing. Similar to SRT, SpR also offers Review classes for individuals who have successfully completed the SpR class.

It's important to note that while Spiritual Response Therapy and Spiritual Restructuring can contribute positively to overall well-being, they are not intended as substitutes for professional medical care. These modalities work in conjunction with a balanced approach to good health and should be used as complementary tools. Always consult with healthcare providers before making any changes to medications or treatment plans.

Spiritual Response Therapy provides a unique and effective method for individuals to release negative programming, explore past life energies, and achieve personal transformation. Through this practice, many have experienced profound shifts, overcoming self-defeating patterns, achieving better health, and fostering harmonious relationships. With its empowering techniques and global availability, Spiritual Response Therapy continues to assist individuals in their journey toward self-discovery, healing, and a more joyful existence.

*In the labyrinth of life, a soul finds guidance.*

## FAQs for Spiritual Response Therapy (SRT)

### Q: What is Spiritual Response Therapy (SRT)?

1. A: SRT is a holistic healing technique that aims to identify and release negative energies, beliefs, and patterns that may be impacting a person's life. By addressing and clearing these energies, SRT seeks to facilitate personal growth, self-awareness, and overall healing.

### Q: How does SRT work?

2. A: SRT practitioners use a pendulum and a set of charts to access the client's subconscious mind and spiritual energies. Through this process, the practitioner identifies and clears the negative energies or programs that may be causing difficulties in the client's life.

## Q: What issues can SRT help with?

3. A: SRT can help with a variety of issues, including emotional, mental, physical, and spiritual well-being. It is particularly useful for addressing energetic blocks stemming from past lives' subconscious memories and vows, which may be impacting personal growth and prosperity.

## Q: How long does an SRT session typically take?

4. A: The duration of an SRT session may vary depending on the individual's needs and the practitioner's approach. Generally, sessions take between 60 to 90 minutes.

## Q: How many sessions will I need?

5. A: The number of sessions required varies for each individual, as it depends on the complexity of the issues being addressed and the client's responsiveness to the therapy. Some clients may experience significant improvement after just one session, while others may require multiple sessions for optimal results. While some clients notice a difference within a day, others' souls and/or subconscious may take longer to process the changes. Either way, changes will happen, whether it be apparent right away or gradual and subtle over a period of weeks or months, friends and relatives will see the differences even though the client hasn't recognized anything different has happened.

## Q: Is SRT a religious practice?

6. A: No, SRT is not a religious practice. It is a spiritual healing technique that focuses on the connection between the individual's energy and overall well-being. People from various religious and spiritual backgrounds can benefit from SRT without compromising their beliefs.

## Q: Can SRT be used alongside traditional medical treatments?

7. A: Yes, SRT is a complementary therapy and can be used in conjunction with traditional medical treatments. However, it is essential to consult with a healthcare professional before beginning any alternative therapy and to continue following their advice throughout the process.

## Q: Are there any side effects or risks associated with SRT?

8. A: SRT is generally considered safe and non-invasive. However, some individuals may experience temporary emotional or physical symptoms as the body adjusts to the release of negative energies. It is always important to communicate with your practitioner about any concerns you may have during the process.

## Q: Can SRT be performed remotely?

9. A: Yes, SRT can be performed remotely, as the practitioner connects with the client's energy on a spiritual level – we are all connected on a universal/spiritual level, otherwise we wouldn't be able to understand each other. Remote sessions are generally conducted when a client requests an SRT Clearing session via phone, email, or online ordering. The practitioner completes the SRT Clearing, and then emails a report to the client after the SRT Clearing has been completed, thus allowing clients to receive the benefits of SRT from the comfort of their own homes.

(Note: SRT is a therapeutic approach that requires the guidance and expertise of a trained practitioner. It is important to consult with a qualified SRT practitioner to ensure a safe and effective healing process.)

## Case Studies for Spiritual Response Therapy (SRT)

The following case studies have been taken from SRT Clearings done over the past 20 years, and were chosen to provide some variety in the issues involved with various case studies clients. Several of these case studies were done as anonymous requests, under the condition that the recipient would not be told of the SRT Clearing. The reason for this is that often anonymous recipient's egos kick in when they do find out about the SRT Clearing done for their benefit but without their conscious knowledge or conscious consent.

In each case, where an anonymous SRT Clearing is done, the recipient's spirit has been consulted for consent, and the SRT clearing was only done with the recipient's spirit's knowledge and consent. If no consent was received, the SRT Clearing was not done.

## Following are six SRT Clearing case studies:

1. Joe, a financial advisor, had stage 4 cancer and wanted to fly to Ireland to visit friends and relatives to be with them one last time. He boarded the plane for his flight but was taken off the plane because he was too sick to fly.  He was taken to the hospital and was not expected to live overnight. A mutual friend called me and explained the situation and asked for an anonymous SRT Clearing, which was done right away. The next morning Joe woke up in the hospital and felt fine. He was discharged from the hospital and went home to be with his family. Joe lived 2-3 weeks and he was able to say his goodbyes to family and friends at home, before peacefully moving on to be with his soul family.

2. Mary was a senior who had a severe breathing condition, known as adult respiratory disease, which was explained to be a hardening of the lungs. She was in an induced medical coma in an oxygen tent in the hospital. She was using all her remaining energy to barely stay alive. A mutual acquaintance phoned me and asked if I would be able to do an emergency anonymous SRT Clearing for Mary. This was done and the next day, Mary's doctor noticed a significant

improvement in her condition. He reassessed her and re-diagnosed Mary with a less severe respiratory condition. He put her on a lung transplant list and Mary was released from the hospital shortly after, with portable oxygen tanks in tow. Mary's breathing condition improved immensely. Eventually, she didn't need to use oxygen tanks to breathe. She was taken off the lung transplant list and enjoyed a normal life from then on.

3. Bill was a commissioned salesman for years and each year his earnings plateaued at the same level, whether it was May, August, October, or any other month between. I did a full SRT Clearing for Bill and found that he had numerous Vows of Poverty and Blocks to Prosperity. The Vows of Poverty were from past religious lives, and they were able to be canceled. The Blocks to Prosperity were cleared, and Bill's income no longer plateaued. He had spectacular earnings thereafter.

4. Trevor was a winter sports professional who had suffered a serious crash on the mountain and was in a coma in the hospital. Although Trevor was not known personally by me, I felt a compelling urgency to assist. I checked with Trevor's spirit and got permission to do an SRT Clearing for him. During the SRT Clearing, I intuitively saw that Trevor would recover consciousness within a few days and would fully recover within a few months. A year after the accident, there was an interview on the radio with Trevor's sister. She was telling what happened after the accident; what she related paralleled what was intuitively picked up when the SRT Clearing

was done. Trevor recovered fully and resumed his career in his sport.

5. Sam was a handyman who was doing some repairs on my house. Sam asked me to do an SRT Clearing for him, which I did. A few days later, Sam told me that his cousin, in her late teens, who was living with him and his wife, was involved with some people who were using drugs and that he was concerned for her since he was responsible for looking after her. I agreed to do an anonymous SRT Clearing for his cousin after he agreed never to tell her. I did the SRT Clearing for Sam's cousin and a few weeks later, Sam called to say that after the SRT Clearing for his cousin, she came home one day and told Sam that she had ceased being around the people who were using drugs. She found some new friends who were much better influences on her.

6. Sarah and Reg were from another city and had come for SRT Clearings for each of them, then asked to have an anonymous SRT Clearing for their teenage daughter. The daughter was having some independence issues and was being a little rebellious, not taking care of herself as much as she had when she was younger. The SRT Clearings were done for Sarah and Reg and for their daughter, Tess. Sarah emailed me a few days after they returned home and found that Tess had cleaned and tidied her room while they were away, even though nothing had been said to Tess about it before they came for their SRT Clearings. Tess settled down and became a model student for the rest of her high school years, then went on to university to become an accountant.

## Sample Spiritual Response Therapy (SRT) Clearing:

The following is a sample SRT Clearing, which was done for the general benefit of the readers of *The Calm Within.* The client has been chosen randomly by Spirit, to be a person who has been suffering from trauma, which is somewhat related to what PTSD (Post Traumatic Stress Disorder) sufferers experience. No other details are known by the author or anyone else, except Spirit and the random person chosen by Spirit for this sample SRT Clearing. For this SRT Clearing, the client will be referred to by the name Roger.

## Here are the steps I follow in doing a general SRT Clearing for a client:

First of all, I cleared both the client and myself to work with "Prep to Work". This is a general clearing preparation so I can get down to the more serious stuff. I do a check on what the conditions were before the "Prep to Work": I check for discarnates, extra souls, number of programs, how many lives the client has had, and how many times the client's soul has been on Earth, the number of Archetypes, Scarring, and number of links in the client's High Self chain (the H/S has a H/S, has a H/S, etc.). I cleared all the links in the client's H/S chain to the level "Above Radiant Love" (as high as possible). I also ask that the number of links in the client's H/S chain be reduced to the ideal/optimum, which is 2 or 3. I also clear the client to the "Void". I also check that the client has been cleared through all nine stacks of SRT charts.

I ask to clear: subconscious clutter, world energies, curses, vows, and soul programs - fatigue, fear of life, frustration, hate, guilt, hate of men, hate of women, hate of God, hate of life, hate of self, health abuse, illness, injustice, intolerance, jealousy, failure, resentment, restlessness, depression, negativity, self-destruction, self-limitation, unworthiness, unforgiveness, unhappiness, judgmental, selfishness, self-centeredness, revenge, and all other issues that are known and unknown.

Then I ask if there is a "Program to Clear", and usually there are one, two, or three "programs" that come forward to be cleared (one at a time). This/these program(s) are more or less sacrificial and when they are cleared the rest go too - like dominoes. After asking if there is a program to clear, and getting a "yes" answer, I ask which chart it is on and I go to that chart and check which program(s) there are that need to be cleared. I get the names of the program(s). Next, I ask when the program(s) were established - most of the time it's Past Lives (95%), after that, I ask who were the main characters in this life, beginning with the client. Usually, there are only 2 characters, but sometimes there are 3 or 4, depending on what is going on with the program or life in that time frame.

Next, I asked if there was any harm. After this, I asked who was harmed and who did the harm. I asked what the harm was - physical, mental, or emotional. Following this, I determined if it was simple, serious, or death. If there is anything else to ask, I get that information and check to see if there was any other hurt or harm, and if there was, I research that and continue until I have found all the hurt or harm in that life between the main characters involved. Sometimes, I get some intuitive information about what was going on, reflecting on all the information I have received so far, and I will check to see if that is correct and if it's I report what I picked up. I then check to see if there is enough information to clear the life, and if there is I clear it. Next, I check to see if there is enough information to clear the program, and if there is I do that also. I check to see if there are any duplicates or sets of duplicates or if there is anything left to rebuild the program, and if there is I clear those items until all is cleared. I check to see how many lives this program was carried forward by the client, and if it is being continued in this life. After this, I check to see if there is another program to clear, and if there is, I do all the steps to clear that program, and I continue until all the sacrificial programs are cleared. I do a cross-check to make sure that there isn't anything that is hidden, or that the soul isn't lying, and make sure that there isn't anything else that needs clearing that didn't come up. I check to see that there is only one soul in the body, and to what age the "inner child" is cleared to (i.e., to what age in the client's life that all the programs are cleared to - usually 112 - 124).

Next, I check to see that all 22 sets of Soul programs in the Etheric body are cleared, that the DNA and chromosomes are all harmonized to the body, that all programs (called "Trailers") are cleared from the DNA, and that Brain Cell Restructuring is or isn't needed. If any of this work is required, I do that. I also check to see if the person needs to be harmonically balanced, and if they do, I ask that they be cleared and baptized by the Holy Spirit and to correct any musical score that is not harmonized. I check to see if the Spirit Body needs clearing, and if it does, I clear it. If there has been any scarring, I clear that. Scarring is a belief that the Soul was ripped away from Source when it was created, and virtually everyone has scarring. Finally, I check to make sure that there are no programs or discarnates and make sure that there is only one Soul in the body.

## That is basically what Spiritual Response Therapy involves.

Discarnates are defined as Souls that have not made it to the Light within the 90-hour limit from the time they died as physical beings on Earth till the time they should have gone to the Light. Discarnates might be "Earthbound" because they are addicted to a place, person, thing, substance, etc. or they may not know that they are dead, they may be afraid to go to the Light because they fear repercussions from someone who they have hurt or harmed, or they may stay around to "help" a loved one. In any case, they need to go to the Light, and when the clearing work is done, they are gone to the Light. Discarnates can have a negative effect or influence on some people, and when they are gone a person's life improves for that reason alone. Extra Souls can be there with the host's permission because they all know that they are going to get cleared when the host gets cleared. Extra Souls can be addicted and/or the host Soul can be addicted to the Extra Soul – sometimes there are double addictions.

**Here is a summary of the findings for the client in this sample SRT Clearing;**

Before Prep to Work [After Clearing]
Number of Discarnates – 72,311,481 [Cleared to 0]
Number of Souls – 3 [Cleared down to 1]
Number of Programs – 71,238 [Cleared to 0]
Number of Lives – 366,666 (older soul)
Number of Times Soul has been on Earth - 92
Archetypes – 81,268 [Cleared to 0]
Scarring - 98 [Cleared to 0]
Links in High Self Chain - 63 [Reduced to 2]

## (1)

Q - Is there a Program to clear? - Yes

Q - What Chart is it on? – Chart #10B – "Programs Created by Spirit"

Q - What is the Program? - "Spiritual Virus"

Q - When was it established? - Past Lives

Q - Characters? – Husband; Wife.

Q - Was there any hurt or harm? – Yes

1: Wife did Simple Emotional Harm to Herself

2: Husband did Emotional Harm to Wife, resulting in Suicide by the Wife

3: Husband did Physical Harm to Himself resulting in Suicide

Q - Can this life be cleared? Yes.  This life was cleared 100%

No intuitive information came up about this life.

Q - Can this program be cleared? Yes.  This program was cleared 100%

There were no duplicate programs or sets of duplicates, and there was nothing left to rebuild the program.

Q - How many lives did this program carry through? – 15 ½ (The ½ is this life).

## (2)

Q - Is there a Program to clear? - Yes

Q - What Chart is it on? – Chart #6A – "Master Programs, Discordant Energy"

Q - What is the Program? - "Self Limitation"

Q - When was it established? - Past Lives

Q - Characters? – Wife #1; Wife #2; There were 2 wives in a lesbian relationship.

Q - Was there any hurt or harm? – Yes

1: Wife #1 did Simple Emotional Harm to Herself

2: Wife #1 did Simple Emotional Harm to Wife #2

3: Wife #2 did Emotional Harm to Herself, resulting in Suicide

3: Wife #1 did Emotional Harm to Herself resulting in Suicide

Q - Can this life be cleared? Yes.  This life was cleared 100%

No intuitive information came up about this life.

Q - Can this program be cleared? Yes.  This program was cleared 100%

There were no duplicate programs or sets of duplicates, and there was nothing left to rebuild the program.

Q - How many lives did this program carry through? – 28 (No ½ life for this program).

Q - Is there a Program to clear? – No

There were no other programs to clear at this point, and I began the cross-check list.

One additional clearing issue came up while doing the Cross-Check List, which referenced Chart #1. The item was "Subconscious Mind". The Subconscious Mind was cleared and purified, per the protocol which was intuitively received.

Roger's Inner Child is cleared of major programs to age 112

All 22 Sets of Soul Programs in the Etheric Body were cleared. 0 Sets of Soul Programs in the Etheric Body needed to be cleared

All 22 sets of Soul Programs in the Etheric Body were cleared.

There are now: 0 discarnates; 1 Soul in the body; and 0 programs – Roger is basically cleared with respect to Past Lives, Other Lives, Other Dimensions, Etc.

## "NOTES":

Blocks are matters that we have a tendency to repress, hide, or downplay. This is because we have been hurt or harmed for expressing them in past lives, so our subconscious protects us from being hurt or harmed in this life, by blocking our expression of these matters. For instance, expressing one's "Intelligence" in past lives resulted in being hurt, harmed, imprisoned, persecuted, ridiculed, belittled, and bullied, hence the subconscious mind protects us from these things in this life. However, this may or may not be the case in this life (maybe in the total number of Programs). These blocks can hinder us from the full expression of our full abilities and capabilities. Once the blocks are gone, we often find that things we hesitated to do become easy and fun, and our lives become much easier and more cheerful.

I did not pick up on any other issues to look at this point and all the clearing work was completed for Roger.

The information around the above-mentioned programs may mean something to the client or it may not. **The main thing to focus on is being cleared** and moving into the future with that in mind.

In general terms, the client may notice positive changes happening in many areas of their life. It may be obvious or it could be subtle. It may happen right away or it may take a period of time. The client may feel lighter, with less stress, and will enjoy many things more fully that they are already enjoying. The client may notice the beauty in everyday things that they may not have been aware of before. There will be changes that will open up, allowing more good to come into their life. The client may not see these changes happening themself, but other people might. It will make their life happier and easier in many ways.

Know that the client is clearer and that changes are now happening. I suggest that after having read this email once or twice, the client put it aside for a while and allow the soul to re-configure itself on its own.  Try to avoid analyzing the research and clearing work. Allow healing to occur naturally. Life will change!  Occasionally they can review where they are, the changes they have noticed since this date, and the SRT clearing work that has been done.

Minor issues may come up from time to time, and that is what life is all about.

Clients are requested to let me know if they notice any changes or have any questions relating to any changes that they experience.

I attach a copy of the Daily Clearing Prayer with the email that I send each client with their SRT Clearing results and notes. Clients are instructed to read it once or twice a day for 4-6 days, thereafter when they feel they need a quick clearing, the client just says the words "Spirit, do the Updated Daily Clearing Prayer for me now - So be it, So it is, Make it so." and it will be done. Self-clearing can be done as often as a client likes. Personally, I am clearing myself all the time.

As a note to the reader, when an SRT Clearing is done for a client, there are many other souls which are also cleared simultaneously. For this sample SRT Clearing, there were an additional 62,611 souls which were cleared.

## About Brooks Allisen

My name is Brooks Allisen, and since 2000, I've been a passionate practitioner in the field of Spiritual Response Therapy (SRT) and Spiritual Restructuring (SpR). My journey into this transformative healing technique began when a fellow practitioner introduced me to SRT. After experiencing a profound clearing session with Robert Detzler, the founder of SRT, I decided to delve deeper into this practice and become certified as an instructor of SRT and SpR.

At the core of my practice, I focus on helping clients remove energetic blocks stemming from past lives and memories. These blocks often manifest as obstacles in various aspects of life, such as prosperity and personal growth. I've had the honor of clearing clients of prosperity blocks and vows of poverty, enabling them to unlock their full potential and embrace a life of abundance.

Through my extensive experience in both SRT and Spiritual Restructuring, I am dedicated to empowering my clients on their journey toward healing, self-awareness, and success. I encourage you to learn more about the power of SRT to unlock the limitless possibilities of your true self.

## Summary of Chapter 2:

"The Calm Within" unveils the wonders of Spiritual Response Therapy (SRT) in its second chapter, providing readers with an enlightening path to emotional liberation. SRT is a powerful modality that addresses past traumas and negative belief systems, offering individuals an opportunity to embrace inner peace and unleash their true potential.

Within the realm of SRT, readers will discover ten profound effects that can significantly impact those grappling with trauma, anxiety, and fear:

Healing Trauma: SRT provides a gentle and effective approach to addressing and healing trauma at its core, empowering individuals to move forward with strength and resilience.

Emotional Liberation: By identifying and clearing negative psychological programs, SRT liberates individuals from self-sabotaging patterns, breaking free from the shackles of fear, anxiety, and limiting beliefs.

Overcoming Anxiety: SRT offers a transformative pathway to alleviate anxiety by addressing its root causes, allowing individuals to experience a heightened sense of calm and tranquility.

Releasing Fear: SRT gently releases deep-rooted fears that hinder personal growth, opening the doors to cultivating courage and self-empowerment.

Restoring Inner Peace: By clearing psychological programs, SRT restores inner peace and harmony, leading to a sense of balance and alignment in daily life.

Enhancing Emotional Resilience: SRT empowers individuals to build emotional resilience by addressing and clearing past wounds and negative patterns, easing their navigation through life's challenges.

Cultivating Self-Awareness: SRT facilitates a journey of self-awareness and self-discovery by exploring the subconscious mind and uncovering hidden beliefs.

Releasing Limiting Beliefs: SRT identifies and releases limiting beliefs, empowering individuals to embrace their full potential and bask in a life of abundance and fulfillment.

Restoring Trust and Confidence: Through the clearing of destructive programs, SRT helps rebuild trust in oneself and one's abilities, restoring confidence and authenticity.

Cultivating Spiritual Connection: SRT nurtures a deepened spiritual connection, guiding individuals to explore higher realms of consciousness and discover profound purpose and meaning.

As readers gain insights into how programs from past lives are carried forward into the present, they embark on a transformative journey of emotional liberation. The enlightening power of SRT allows individuals to release negative energies, delve into past life influences, and embrace a life filled with empowerment and serenity.

*"Strength from Within"*

*In life's harsh winds, we firmly stand,*
*With unwavering strength, hand in hand.*
*Adversity's test, a challenge to endure,*
*But within our hearts, the cure is sure.*

*Breathe, relax, and let go.*

# Biomagnetic Pair Therapy Helps Resolve Emotional Blocks/Issues

"Feelings are much like waves, we can't stop them from coming but we can choose which ones to surf."

- Jonatan Martensson

*Balance your energy, ride life's waves gracefully.*

## Balancing Energy Pathways: The Power of Biomagnetic Pair Therapy

In the realm of natural therapies for healing trauma, anxiety, stress, and fear, Biomagnetic Pair Therapy (BMP) stands out as a powerful and innovative approach. Offering a gentle yet effective method, BMP has gained recognition for its ability to identify unresolved emotions and promote inner harmony. In this chapter, we delve into what Biomagnetic Pair Therapy is, its history, the impact of its practice, and the pivotal role of Dr. Luis F. Garcia in developing, practicing, and teaching this transformative therapy. The human body generates its own magnetic field as atoms exchange electrical charges within our cells. We are alive with electrical and magnetic energy.

## What is Biomagnetic Pair Therapy?

Biomagnetic Pair Therapy, also known as Biomagnetic Therapy, is a non-invasive and natural healing modality that focuses on restoring balance to the body's internal environment. It revolves around the concept of restoring electromagnetic balance which creates an environment that inhibits and restores function and pathogens, which are microorganisms that can cause disease or imbalances within the body. These pathogens can be bacteria, viruses, fungi, mold, or parasites.

In BMP, it is believed that imbalances in the body foster pathogens which can contribute to various health conditions and emotional disturbances. The therapy involves the strategic placement of magnets on specific points to restore balance and neutralize pathogens, promoting the body's innate ability to heal itself.

## A Brief History of Biomagnetic Pair Therapy

Biomagnetic Pair Therapy traces its origins to the pioneering work of Dr. Isaac Goiz Durán, a Mexican medical doctor. Dr. Goiz dedicated several decades to researching and developing this therapy, inspired by his vision of offering a non-invasive and effective approach to healing.

Dr. Goiz's research led to the discovery of specific Biomagnetic pairs that, when balanced, could aid in the restoration of health and emotional well-being. His groundbreaking work sparked a revolutionary shift in the field of natural medicine, leading to the establishment of Biomagnetic Pair Therapy as a respected healing modality.

## The Impact of Biomagnetic Pair Therapy

The impact of Biomagnetic Pair Therapy has been profound, attracting the attention of healthcare professionals and individuals seeking alternative approaches to healing. This therapy has demonstrated success in addressing various health conditions, including emotional imbalances associated with trauma, anxiety, stress, and fear.

Countless individuals have experienced positive outcomes from BMP, reporting a reduction in symptoms, improved emotional well-being, and a greater sense of inner calm and resilience. As more people seek alternatives to conventional medicine, Biomagnetic Pair Therapy continues to gain popularity as a gentle and effective option for holistic healing.

## Dr. Luis F. Garcia: The Leading Figure in Biomagnetic Pair Therapy

Central to the development, practice, and dissemination of Biomagnetic Pair Therapy is Dr. Luis F. Garcia. A prominent figure in the field, Dr. Garcia has dedicated his career to advancing this therapy and sharing its benefits with others worldwide.

As a respected practitioner and educator, Dr. Garcia has traveled extensively, offering workshops and training programs to healthcare professionals and individuals interested in learning BMP. His expertise and dedication have helped expand the reach of Biomagnetic Pair Therapy, making it accessible to a broader audience.

## Summary of the Evolution of Biomagnetic Pair Therapy

Biomagnetic Pair Therapy is a powerful natural therapy that holds the potential to address unresolved emotions and promote healing from within. Driven by a rich history and the pioneering work of Dr. Isaac Goiz Durán, BMP has emerged as a transformative modality in healing trauma, anxiety, stress, and fear.

At the forefront of this therapy's advancement is Dr. Luis F. Garcia, whose contributions to developing, practicing, and teaching Biomagnetic Pair Therapy have made a lasting impact. Through this gentle and effective approach, countless individuals have found relief, embracing a sense of serenity and emotional balance.

## Details of the Biomagnetic Pair Therapy Process

Magnets have a North Pole and a South Pole depending on which side or which polarity you use, you can either repel or attract another magnet.

Although we cannot see the magnetic field that these magnets emit, we can certainly observe the effects of the magnetic field as it is able to affect the magnetic field in a specific area.

This will push around molecules because of the magnetic stimulus on ions and can cause the pH of a liquid to change. The magnitude of change is an indirect consequence of the mineral content.

When strong magnets are placed over a body part that has an acidic pH, it will cause a muscular contraction on one side of the body including the arms and legs.

If, on the contrary, the body part has an alkaline pH and a strong magnet is placed over that particular body part, it will cause muscular relaxation, and we will observe an elongation of that body part.

So, if a person is laying down and you are at the feet, if you place a magnet on a place where there is an imbalance, you will notice that that one leg will become elongated and be longer than the other. Once you place a magnet of opposite polarity on the corresponding scan point, the legs will rebalance and return to equal length. The magnets are left on the client for a specified amount of time in order for the magnetic energy to work and do what is needed to do throughout the whole body.

During a typical session, a therapist may identify and place many pairs. A session typically lasts approximately 90 minutes, during which, it is normal to feel some different or weird sensations traveling on or along the body.

As the magnets are placed at different points the client may feel either some numbness, cold sensations, or tingling sensations due to the movement of the molecules throughout the body.

These sensations usually last for a few minutes, and then dissipate.

The client may also feel tired after the session.

It's very similar to going to the gym if a person hasn't worked out in over six months and they go back to the gym.

The first day, while they're at the gym, they feel great, but the next day or for the next two days, they're going to feel tired.

In the same way that they may feel tired after a full Biomagnetic Pair Therapy experience.

And, just like going to the gym, after that first initial visit to the gym, a person can't expect to wake up the next day and have a much better body or more energy.

It may take about one to three weeks after having been to the gym before a person can start to realize all of the benefits in their body.

The same exact thing happens with Biomagnetic Pair Therapy. Many people feel results immediately, but for some, it may take a few days or even weeks for a person to feel the impact of the magnets. The body needs time to adjust, get rid of pathogens, and rebalance itself.

Once again, Biomagnetism or Biomagnetic Pair Therapy involves the placement of pairs of magnets to correct or balance pH issues in the body that will re-establish the normal structure and function of our bodies.

Biomagnetic Pair Therapy should not be confused with traditional magnetic therapy. Magnetic therapy is used internationally and by medical doctors. Magnetic therapy uses one polarity and the magnets are low strength. Biomagnetic Pair Therapy which uses negative and positive (two) polarities and the magnets are high strength.

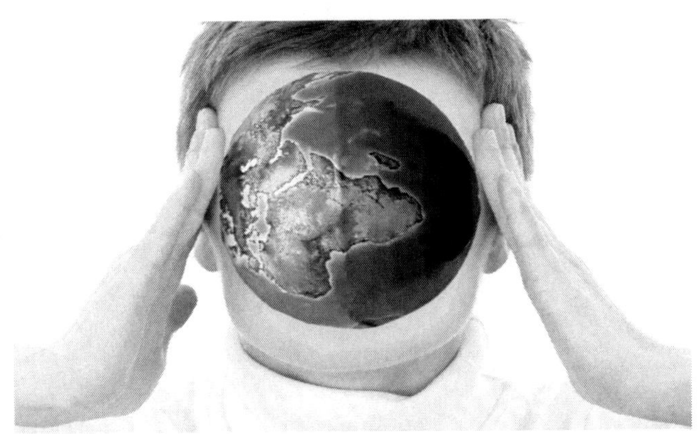

*Experience the magnetic pull to tranquility.*

## Traumas that Biomagnetic Pair Therapy Can Effectively Address

In the world of natural therapies, Biomagnetic Pair Therapy shines as a powerful tool to address various traumas, anxieties, fears, and negative emotions. This gentle yet effective approach can significantly impact individuals' emotional well-being, offering relief and inner harmony. Here are ten types of challenges that Biomagnetic Pair Therapy may effectively address:

Childhood Trauma

Relationship Traumas

Work-Related Stress

Anxiety Disorders

Phobias

Post-Traumatic Stress Disorder (PTSD)

Grief and Loss

Performance Anxiety

Social Anxiety

Emotional Resilience

Through the strategic placement of magnets on specific Biomagnetic Pair locations, this therapy aims to identify unresolved emotions and restore balance to the body's internal environment helping the body to process the issues. By addressing the root causes of traumas, anxieties, fears, and negative emotions, Biomagnetic Pair Therapy empowers individuals to embark on a journey of emotional healing and inner serenity.

## Sample Biomagnetic Pair Therapy Session

Following is a sample Biomagnetic Pair Therapy session, which is done for the general benefit of the readers of *The Calm Within*. The client has been chosen randomly by Spirit, to be a person who has been suffering from one of the types of traumas listed above. No other details are known by the author or anyone else, except Spirit and the random person chosen by Spirit for this sample Biomagnetic Pair Therapy session. For this Biomagnetic Pair Therapy session, the client will be referred to by the name Angela.

Angela is experiencing anxiety disorders.

There are 250 Biomagnetic Pairs that were scanned from the charts which are from the BIOMAGNETISM AND BEYOND; TRAINING SEMINAR LEVEL 1 & 2, Presented by Dr. Luis F. Garcia, October 10-14, 2022 in San Antonio TX. Dr. Garcia scanned through the scan sheet provided at the seminar using muscle testing via an ideomotor response technique.

There were 10 Biomagnetic Pairs that were active, indicating several imbalances for Angela. Pairs of Biomagnetic Neodymium Magnets were placed on a mannequin in the locations given in the charts. A mannequin is used as a surrogate for the client when Biomagnetic Pair Therapy sessions are done remotely. The advantages of using the mannequin for remote sessions are: the client doesn't need to travel to the session; the client does not need to take time from their busy schedule for a session; the mannequin doesn't get tired or need to go to the bathroom or need a drink of water during a session; the client can be anywhere on the globe when sessions are done. After the session is completed, the Biomagnetism therapist can email the client photos of the session, showing the placement of the magnets and a PDF copy of the Biomagnetic Pairs placed in the session, which would give detailed information on each of the Biomagnetic Pairs, along with the Pathogen/Condition and Interpretation associated with each of the Biomagnetic Pairs.

It should be noted that each client is scanned using all 250 Biomagnetic Pairs, for all conditions that are affecting the client, not just for conditions that are directly related to the conditions the client is noticing symptoms for. This is a holistic process that makes sure that underlying health issues are addressed. This is the case for the sample Biomagnetic Pair Therapy remote session for Angela.

Dr. Luis F. Garcia's Level I and Level II Scan Sheet is divided into 10 categories. In the Emotional Pairs category, however, there were no Biomagnetic Pairs that were needed for

Angela. Seemingly unrelated symptoms, especially if there are multiple symptoms, can cause anxiety for a client, and if some or all the symptoms are not addressed at their root, the client may suffer from a heightened level of anxiety, which may manifest to the level of an anxiety disorder. This seemed to be the situation for Angela. Below is the list of Biomagnetic Pairs that were detected to address imbalances for Angela.

Scapula - Scapula
Cranial - Cranial
Lacrimal Duct - Lacrimal Duct
Tonsil - Tonsil
Temporal (L) - Temporal (L)
Thymus - Thymus
Liver - Pylorus
Deltoid Insertion - Delta Insertion
Vas Deferens - Larynx
Popliteal Fossa - Popliteal Fossa

Angela's experience with Biomagnetic Pair Therapy yielded impressive results. Following her initial session, there was an immediate 75% reduction in her anxiety levels. Over the following three months, Angela's results were periodically tested and showed a progressive reduction to 95% overall. This left Angela with a profound sense of calm and well-being, showcasing the effectiveness of Biomagnetic Pair Therapy in reducing anxiety.

Below are photos showing of the placement of the Biomagnetic Pairs on the mannequin. The length of time for the magnets to remain in place on the mannequin was determined to be two hours, again, using an ideomotor response technique by the author of this book.

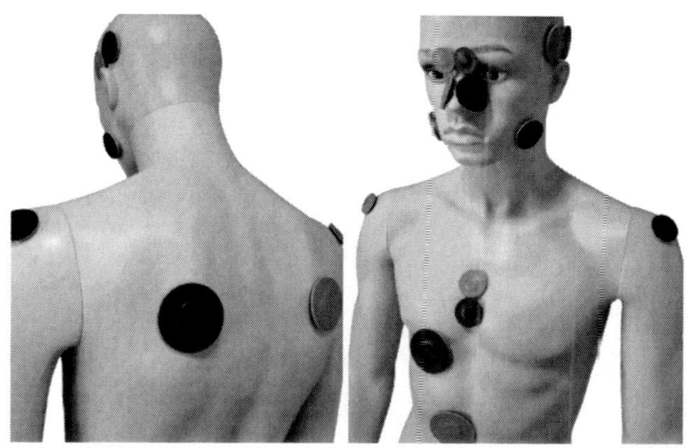

*Bio Magnetic Pairs Therapy Working Remotely*

## Summary of Chapter 3:

In the world of natural therapies, Biomagnetic Pair Therapy shines as a powerful tool to address various traumas, anxieties, fears, and negative emotions. This gentle yet effective approach can significantly impact individuals' emotional well-being, offering relief and inner harmony. Here are ten types of challenges that Biomagnetic Pair Therapy can effectively address.

Childhood Trauma

Relationship Traumas

Work-Related Stress

Anxiety Disorders

Phobias

Post-Traumatic Stress Disorder (PTSD)

Grief and Loss

Performance Anxiety

Social Anxiety

Emotional Resilience

Through the strategic placement of magnets on specific Biomagnetic pairs scan points on the body, this therapy aims to identify and address and restore balance to the body's internal environment. By addressing the root causes of traumas, anxieties, fears, and negative emotions, Biomagnetic Pair Therapy empowers individuals to embark on a journey of emotional healing and inner serenity.

In this list, we have outlined ten types of traumas, anxieties, fears, and negative emotions that Biomagnetic Pair Therapy can effectively address, offering hope and relief to those seeking emotional healing and well-being.

# Natural Supplements Build Healthy Neurological Pathways

"Eating healthy food fills your body with energy and nutrients. Imagine your cells smiling back at you and saying: 'Thank you!'"

– Karen Salmanshon

*Nourish your body, nuture your calmness.*

## Unlocking the Potential of Natural Supplements for Emotional Healing: Building Healthy Neurological Pathways

In the fast-paced and demanding world we live in, navigating the complexities of life can sometimes take a toll on our emotional well-being. Dealing with trauma, anxiety, stress, fears, and negative emotions is an intricate process that requires a multifaceted approach. Natural supplements, encompassing a diverse array of herbs; vitamins; minerals; amino acids; enzymes; concentrated vegetable-fruit-fiber-spice powders; and nutrition bars, have emerged as powerful allies in supporting emotional healing and building healthy neurological pathways.

## The Connection Between Nutrition and Emotional Well-being

Before delving into specific supplements, it's essential to understand the profound connection between nutrition and emotional well-being. The human brain, a complex network of neurons and neurotransmitters, relies on various nutrients to function optimally. Neurotransmitters, the brain's chemical messengers, play a pivotal role in regulating mood, emotions, and cognitive function.

Many neurotransmitters are synthesized from dietary precursors derived from proteins, fats, and carbohydrates. For example, serotonin, often referred to as the "happy neurotransmitter," is synthesized from the amino acid tryptophan found in protein-rich foods. Similarly, omega-3 fatty acids, commonly found in fish and certain nuts, are crucial for maintaining healthy brain function and supporting cognitive abilities.

## Stress and the Adrenal Glands

Stress, a prevalent aspect of modern life, can have profound effects on our emotional well-being. When stress levels rise, the adrenal glands release cortisol, the primary stress hormone. In small doses, cortisol is essential for maintaining balance and regulating various bodily processes. However, chronic stress can lead to an overproduction of cortisol, which can negatively impact emotional health.

## Ashwagandha (Withania somnifera): The Adaptogen for Stress Management

Ashwagandha, an adaptogenic herb from Ayurvedic medicine, has gained significant popularity for its stress-reducing properties. As an adaptogen, ashwagandha helps the body adapt to stressors, promoting a state of balance and reducing the impact of stress on the body and mind. Studies have shown that ashwagandha can lower cortisol levels and improve perceived stress and anxiety levels in individuals experiencing chronic stress.

## Rhodiola (Rhodiola rosea): A Resilience-Boosting Herb

Rhodiola, another adaptogenic herb, is renowned for its ability to enhance resilience and combat stress-related fatigue. This herb supports the body's stress response by moderating cortisol levels and reducing feelings of burnout and exhaustion. By enhancing the body's ability to cope with stress, Rhodiola may also contribute to improved mood and emotional well-being.

## Anxiety and the GABA Connection

GABA (Gamma-Aminobutyric Acid) is a neurotransmitter that plays a crucial role in calming the nervous system and reducing anxiety. GABA acts as a natural tranquilizer, inhibiting excessive nerve impulses that can lead to feelings of anxiety and restlessness.

## L-Theanine: The Relaxation Amino Acid

L-Theanine, an amino acid found in green tea, is known for its relaxation-inducing effects. By promoting the production of alpha brainwaves, L-theanine induces a state of relaxed alertness, which can ease feelings of stress and anxiety.

## Valerian Root (Valeriana officinalis): A Calming Herb

Valerian root has been used for centuries as an herbal remedy for insomnia and anxiety. It contains compounds that interact with GABA receptors in the brain, promoting relaxation and aiding in the management of anxiety and sleep disturbances.

## Passionflower (Passiflora incarnata): Easing Anxiety and Promoting Sleep

Passionflower is a gentle herb often used to alleviate anxiety, restlessness, and insomnia. It helps increase GABA levels in the brain, leading to a calming effect and improved sleep quality.

## Mood Regulation and Brain Health

Omega-3 fatty acids are essential for supporting brain health and mood regulation. They are integral components of cell membranes in the brain and play a crucial role in neurotransmitter function. DHA (docosahexaenoic acid) and EPA (eicosapentaenoic acid), two types of omega-3s, are particularly beneficial for emotional well-being.

## St. John's Wort (Hypericum perforatum): Nature's Antidepressant

St. John's Wort is an herbal remedy widely recognized for its antidepressant effects. It contains active compounds that inhibit the reuptake of serotonin, norepinephrine, and dopamine, promoting a positive mood and emotional balance.

## Saffron Extract (Crocus sativus): A Natural Mood Enhancer

Saffron, a prized spice, has demonstrated antidepressant effects in research studies. Its active compounds, including crocin and safranal, influence neurotransmitters in the brain, contributing to enhanced mood and emotional well-being.

## B Vitamins: Essential for Emotional Resilience

B vitamins, including B6 and B12, are crucial for the synthesis of neurotransmitters involved in emotional regulation. These vitamins play a key role in converting amino acids into serotonin and other mood-stabilizing neurotransmitters, supporting emotional resilience and overall well-being.

## Magnesium: Nervous System Support

Magnesium, a vital mineral, is involved in over 300 biochemical reactions in the body, including those related to the nervous system. It helps calm the nervous system and alleviate symptoms of nervous tension and irritability.

## Melatonin and Sleep Support

Melatonin, a hormone produced by the pineal gland, is responsible for regulating sleep-wake cycles. Supplementing with melatonin can help individuals struggling with sleep disturbances, promoting restful sleep and overall emotional well-being.

## Balancing Gut Health for Emotional Resilience

The gut-brain axis is a bidirectional communication network connecting the gut and the brain. A healthy gut microbiome is essential for balanced mood and emotional resilience.

## Probiotics: Nurturing the Gut Microbiome

Probiotics are live beneficial bacteria that support gut health and overall well-being. They help maintain a diverse and balanced gut microbiome, positively impacting mood and emotional health.

## Prebiotics: Feeding the Beneficial Bacteria

Prebiotics are non-digestible fibers that serve as food for probiotics, helping them thrive in the gut. By nourishing the beneficial bacteria, prebiotics contribute to a flourishing gut microbiome and, in turn, support emotional resilience.

## Holistic Approach to Emotional Healing

While natural supplements offer significant support for emotional healing, they are most effective when integrated into a holistic approach to well-being. Lifestyle factors, such as regular exercise, balanced nutrition, sufficient sleep, mindfulness practices, and supportive relationships, play essential roles in emotional well-being.

## Seeking Professional Guidance

It is vital to remember that every individual is unique and emotional challenges may stem from various factors. While natural supplements can be beneficial, it is crucial to consult with a qualified healthcare professional before beginning any supplementation regimen, especially if taking medications or experiencing chronic health conditions.

*Elevate your spirits, naturally.*

## Summary of Chapter 4:

Natural supplements provide valuable support for building healthy neurological pathways and fostering emotional well-being. When incorporated into a comprehensive wellness plan that addresses diet, lifestyle, and emotional health, these supplements can play a transformative role in overcoming trauma, anxiety, stress, fears, and negative emotions. By nourishing the body and mind, individuals can embrace a renewed sense of inner calm, serenity, and emotional balance—the foundation for "The Calm Within."

*Cultivate calmness among the blossoms of life.*

# Meditation and Relaxation Therapy Calms Nerves and Restores Focus

"The mind is definitely something that can be transformed, and meditation is a means to transform it."

— Dalai Lama

Embark on a journey of stillness and inner tranquility through meditation and relaxation therapy

In the quest for inner peace and emotional healing, meditation, and relaxation therapy stand as powerful allies. As we explore the fifth chapter of "The Calm Within," we embark on a journey into the transformative realm of meditation and relaxation techniques—a journey that holds the promise of calming nerves, restoring focus, and overcoming trauma, anxiety, stress, fears, and negative emotions.

## The Path to Inner Stillness: How to Meditate

Meditation, an ancient practice with roots in diverse spiritual traditions, offers a sanctuary of serenity amidst life's chaos. At its core, meditation involves training the mind to focus and redirect thoughts, promoting a state of heightened awareness and inner stillness.

## The steps to meditation are simple, but the practice itself can be profound:

Find a Quiet Space: Choose a tranquil environment free from distractions. Create a space that feels inviting and peaceful—a sanctuary for your mind to retreat to.

Get Comfortable: Sit or lie down in a comfortable position, allowing your body to relax and release tension. Many find sitting with a straight back and relaxed shoulders to be conducive to meditation.

*Recharge your spirit, embrace the stillness.*

Focus on Your Breath: Close your eyes and bring your attention to your breath. Observe the natural rhythm of your breath as it flows in and out of your body.

Release Thoughts Gently: As thoughts arise, acknowledge them without judgment, and gently redirect your focus back to your breath. Allow thoughts to come and go like passing clouds in the sky.

Embrace the Present Moment: Cultivate mindfulness by being fully present in the moment. Engage your senses and notice the sensations, sounds, and feelings around you.

Practice Regularly: Like any skill, meditation benefits from consistent practice. Start with a few minutes each day and gradually increase the duration as you become more comfortable with the practice.

## Unveiling Meditation Styles: Finding the Right Fit

Meditation offers a vast array of styles, allowing individuals to choose the approach that resonates with their unique preferences and goals. Some common meditation styles include:

Mindfulness Meditation: Emphasizes being fully present and aware of the moment without judgment. It involves observing thoughts and sensations with non-reactive awareness.

Loving-Kindness Meditation: Focuses on cultivating feelings of love, compassion, and kindness towards oneself and others.

Guided Meditation: Involves following a recorded meditation session led by a guide or instructor. This style can be helpful for beginners and those seeking specific intentions.

Transcendental Meditation (TM): Involves the use of a silent, individually assigned mantra to achieve a state of profound rest and relaxation.

Yoga Nidra: A guided relaxation technique that allows deep physical and mental relaxation while maintaining full awareness.

## The Timeless Gift of Patience: How Long Does It Take to Meditate?

The duration of meditation sessions can vary, and there is no definitive timeframe that applies to everyone. Beginners may find it beneficial to start with short sessions, ranging from 5 to 10 minutes, and gradually extend the time as they build their practice.

Ultimately, meditation is a personal journey, and the right duration depends on individual needs and preferences. Some individuals find immense benefit from brief daily meditations, while others may engage in longer sessions for deeper contemplation and reflection.

## The Power of Long-Term Practice: How Meditation and Relaxation Techniques Create Lasting Change

Meditation and relaxation techniques offer more than momentary relief—they hold the potential to create lasting positive changes in the brain and body. Regular practice of meditation has been shown to:

Reduce Stress: Meditation activates the body's relaxation response, lowering cortisol levels and alleviating the physical and mental toll of stress.

Improve Emotional Regulation: By fostering mindfulness and self-awareness, meditation helps individuals navigate and regulate their emotions more effectively.

Enhance Focus and Concentration: Regular meditation improves attention span and cognitive function, sharpening focus and productivity.

Promote Emotional Resilience: Meditation cultivates a sense of inner calm and equanimity, empowering individuals to bounce back from adversity with greater strength.

Boost Immune Function: Lower stress levels and improved well-being from meditation can positively influence the immune system.

Strengthen Neuroplasticity: Meditation has been associated with increased gray matter density in brain regions related to learning, memory, and self-awareness.

## The Inner Landscape: How Meditation and Relaxation Feel

During meditation and relaxation sessions, individuals may experience a range of sensations, thoughts, and emotions.

Some common experiences include:

Inner Calm: A sense of tranquility and peace may envelop the mind, providing a break from the chaos of daily life.

Increased Awareness: As the mind settles, individuals may become more attuned to their thoughts and feelings, fostering self-awareness.

Release of Tension: The body may relax, releasing physical tension and promoting a sense of ease.

Mind Wandering: Thoughts may drift in and out, leading the mind away from the focus on the breath or other anchors.

Restlessness: Especially for beginners, restlessness or impatience may arise. It's essential to embrace these experiences with non-judgment and return to the practice.

Emotional Release: Deep relaxation and mindfulness may bring forth emotions that were previously suppressed, allowing for healthy emotional processing.

## Finding the Optimal Session Length: Striking the Balance

While there are no strict rules on how long a meditation or relaxation session should last, several factors can help individuals find their optimal session length:

Consistency: Consistency in practice is more important than session length. Regular shorter sessions are often more effective than occasional longer sessions.

Comfort: Engaging in meditation and relaxation for a duration that feels comfortable and sustainable is key to building a lasting practice.

Personal Goals: Tailor session lengths to individual intentions and goals. Longer sessions may be suitable for deep introspection, while shorter sessions can offer daily stress relief.

Progression: As meditation skills grow, individuals may naturally gravitate towards longer sessions for more profound experiences.

## A Tapestry of Transformation: The Positive Impact of Meditation and Relaxation

The benefits of meditation and relaxation extend beyond individual practice sessions. By integrating these techniques into daily life, individuals can experience a transformation that ripples throughout their entire being:

Stress Reduction: Consistent practice reduces overall stress levels, enhancing well-being and overall quality of life.

Emotional Regulation: Meditation fosters emotional resilience, helping individuals respond to life's challenges with greater composure.

Improved Relationships: As individuals cultivate inner peace, they become better equipped to engage in harmonious relationships with others.

Enhanced Focus and Productivity: A clear and focused mind boosts productivity and creativity in daily tasks and responsibilities.

Heightened Mindfulness: Greater mindfulness promotes a profound connection to the present moment, enriching experiences and relationships.

Better Sleep: Meditation and relaxation support restful sleep, promoting overall health and vitality.

Self-Discovery: The inner journey of meditation can lead to profound insights and self-discovery.

## Embracing the Practice: How to Overcome Challenges

Meditation and relaxation, like any practice, may present challenges along the way. Some common challenges include

Restlessness: It is natural for the mind to wander during meditation. Gently guide your focus back to your anchor, whether it be the breath or a mantra.

Impatience: Avoid placing expectations on the meditation experience. Embrace each session as it unfolds without judgment.

Mind Chatter: Thoughts may arise persistently. Instead of suppressing them, observe them with detached awareness, allowing them to pass.

Time Constraints: If time is limited, opt for shorter sessions or incorporate mini-meditation breaks throughout the day.

## The Beauty of the Journey: Embracing Meditation and Relaxation for Emotional Healing

Embracing meditation and relaxation techniques opens the door to a profound inner journey—a journey that holds the promise of overcoming trauma, anxiety, stress, fears, and negative emotions. By nurturing inner stillness and mindfulness, individuals can tap into an innate wellspring of peace and resilience. Whether embarking on a journey of self-discovery or seeking emotional healing, meditation, and relaxation serve as transformative tools on the path to "The Calm Within."

In this comprehensive exploration of meditation and relaxation therapy, we have delved into the transformative potential of these practices in calming nerves and restoring focus. From understanding how to meditate and exploring various meditation styles to unveiling the lasting impact of long-term practice, this section aims to provide a roadmap for harnessing the power of meditation and relaxation in overcoming trauma, anxiety, stress, fears, and negative emotions. By embracing these techniques with patience, intention, and an open heart, individuals can embark on a journey of profound inner healing, finding solace and serenity within the depths of their being.

## Sample Guided Meditation

Close your eyes and imagine standing atop a lush green hill on a tropical island. Feel the warm sun on your head and shoulders as gentle breezes sway the long grass around you. Look down the hill and spot a winding path that leads to a small forest, and beyond, the mesmerizing ocean with waves shimmering under the clear blue sky. Slowly, you stroll down the path, the ferns and grasses brushing against your legs, and a faint scent of salt fills the air.

As you move on, the distant sound of the ocean mingles with the faint calls of seabirds. A sense of calmness and tranquility washes over you, making each step feel effortless, like floating on air. The forest envelops you with its soothing embrace - the gentle songs of birds and the woody scent relax you further. You follow the winding path as it leads you closer to the beach, brushing aside foliage until suddenly, the warm sun greets you again, and you find yourself on a beautiful deserted beach.

The golden shoreline stretches invitingly, and you feel the warm sand between your toes as you wander lazily to the water's edge. The sand beneath your feet changes to a cooler moistness near the shoreline, and every so often, larger waves send rivulets of foamy water around your feet. Watching the waves wash over the sand, you notice tiny colored pebbles glinting like jewels in the sunlight. The scent of the ocean, the sound of the water hissing over the sand, and the warmth of the sun create a timeless atmosphere, calming your mind.

As you sit on the beach, you notice a large, fluffy, white cloud appearing on the horizon, rapidly growing bigger until it covers the entire sky above you. Instinctively, you know that you can release all your worries, cares, fears, and anxieties to this cloud. You visualize your worries spiraling away and being absorbed by the cloud until it bursts with sunlight, dispersing all your concerns to the edges of the universe. You are left feeling completely relaxed, without a single care in the world.

Now, in this serene state, you drift off into a deep and peaceful sleep. As you dream, you find yourself walking down a long corridor in the depths of your subconscious mind. Time and space lose their meaning, and the walls of the corridor dissolve, leading you to a room filled with a gentle golden light. In this room, you realize that what you once perceived as limits are actually stepping stones to greater success.

One wall of the room displays words and images, and you understand that your mind is now receptive to positive changes. The word "READY" flashes on the screen, signaling your readiness to accept and act upon the positive suggestions and affirmations that will positively impact your thoughts, feelings, and behaviors in the days, weeks, and months to come.

As you open your eyes, you carry this newfound sense of calm and confidence with you, knowing you have the power to overcome trauma, anxiety, and negative thoughts. You are resilient, and every challenge is just a stepping stone on your path to greater strength and success.

Enjoy the experience you've had with this guided meditation and let your mind find the peace and acceptance in your life and your surroundings that you have been seeking.

**Note to Reader:**

The preceding guided meditation is only to be used in a safe, peaceful setting. Avoid operating any kind of machinery, vehicles, or other mindful tasks while listening to any guided meditations. Your mental focus will be on relaxation, rather than your mental focus being on skills-needed tasks.

## Summary of Chapter 5:

In this transformative chapter of "The Calm Within," the author unravels the art of meditation and relaxation techniques, guiding readers toward emotional liberation. By delving into the intricacies of meditation, they illuminate the path to inner serenity and resilience against life's challenges.

Meditation has become more than just a practice; it has evolved into a vital tool for releasing trauma, anxiety, stress, fears, and negative emotions. The gentle yet profound exploration of different meditation styles and their unique benefits equips readers with a versatile toolkit to embrace stillness, clarity, and emotional restoration.

This chapter is a voyage of self-discovery and empowerment, punctuated by actionable insights on how to meditate effectively, the duration of sessions, and the emotional tapestry one might experience.

The author illuminates the transformative potential of meditation and relaxation therapy, ensuring readers find not just calm, but the resilient core that lies within.

*"Endless Horizon"*

*Through winding paths and challenges unknown,*
*We'll find our way, seeds of strength sown.*
*In the tapestry of life, we each play a part,*
*Toward the endless horizon, with love in our heart.*

*Countryside's whispers soothe your soul.*

# Hypnotherapy Clears Unhealthy Emotions and Resets Feelings of Happiness

"Change Your Mind, Change Your Negative Thoughts. Get Hypnotized today."

- Milton Erickson

## Unlocking Inner Healing: How Hypnotherapy Clears Unhealthy Emotions and Resets Feelings of Happiness

As we journey deeper into the realms of healing trauma, anxiety, stress, fears, and negative emotions, the path of hypnotherapy unfolds—a path that holds the promise of accessing the subconscious mind to unlock profound emotional healing and rediscover happiness. In the sixth chapter of "The Calm Within," we explore the transformative power of hypnotherapy, a gentle yet potent tool for emotional restoration.

## Understanding the State of Hypnosis: Different Types of Hypnosis

*Time to reset, time to find inner peace.*

Hypnosis is a state of focused attention and heightened suggestibility, where the subconscious mind becomes more receptive to positive suggestions and healing insights. Various types of hypnosis exist, each serving unique purposes:

Stage Hypnosis: Often seen as entertainment, stage hypnosis showcases the power of suggestion in a fun and theatrical manner. Participants volunteer to engage in playful hypnosis, demonstrating the mind's potential for altered states.

Hypnotherapy: Distinguished from stage hypnosis, hypnotherapy is a therapeutic modality used to address emotional challenges, break negative patterns, and facilitate personal growth. Hypnotherapy sessions are guided by trained professionals who tailor the experience to the individual's healing needs.

Self-Hypnosis: Self-hypnosis empowers individuals to induce a hypnotic state on their own, through guided recordings or learned techniques. This form of hypnosis can be an invaluable tool for self-improvement and emotional well-being.

Natural Hypnosis: Natural hypnosis occurs spontaneously in our daily lives when our minds enter a focused and suggestible state. This can happen during activities like daydreaming, reading, or driving, allowing the subconscious to process information more deeply.

## Diverse Techniques in Hypnotherapy: Tailoring Healing to Individual Needs

In hypnotherapy, a range of techniques or styles is employed by skilled practitioners to address the unique emotional challenges of each individual. Some common techniques include

Regression Therapy: This technique takes individuals back to past events or experiences to identify and heal unresolved emotions or traumas.

Suggestion Therapy: Positive affirmations and suggestions are used to foster new behaviors and thought patterns.

Parts Therapy: This technique works with conflicting aspects of the subconscious mind to achieve inner harmony and resolution.

Inner Child Work: Healing the wounded inner child by addressing past experiences and nurturing emotional growth.

Gestalt Therapy: Encourages individuals to explore and integrate different parts of their personalities and emotions.

## The Timing of Healing: How Long Does Hypnotherapy Take?

The duration of hypnotherapy varies depending on individual needs and the complexity of the emotional challenges being addressed. Some individuals may experience significant breakthroughs in a few sessions, while others may require more extended treatment for lasting change. The depth of healing is a gradual process that unfolds uniquely for each person.

## Long-Term Effects of Hypnotherapy: Nurturing Inner Transformation

Hypnotherapy holds the potential for lasting positive change, as it accesses the subconscious mind—the root of deep-seated emotions and beliefs. The benefits of hypnotherapy include:

Emotional Release: Hypnotherapy can facilitate the release of suppressed emotions and unresolved traumas, providing emotional catharsis.

Breaking Negative Patterns: By identifying and addressing negative thought patterns, hypnotherapy empowers individuals to break free from self-destructive behaviors.

Stress Reduction: Hypnotherapy induces deep relaxation, reducing stress and promoting emotional well-being.

Enhanced Self-Confidence: Positive suggestions and affirmations can bolster self-esteem and self-confidence.

Phobia and Fear Resolution: Hypnotherapy can help individuals confront and overcome irrational fears and phobias.

Pain Management: Hypnotherapy has been used successfully to manage chronic pain and improve overall physical well-being.

## Into the Hypnotic Realm: How a Hypnotherapy Session Feels

During a hypnotherapy session, individuals experience a state of profound relaxation and focus. While the specific sensations may vary, some common experiences include:

Deep Relaxation: The body and mind enter a state of deep calm and relaxation.

Heightened Awareness: Although deeply relaxed, individuals maintain awareness and control over their thoughts and actions.

Heightened Suggestibility: The subconscious mind becomes more receptive to positive suggestions.

Inner Journey: Hypnotherapy opens a gateway to explore the inner landscape of the subconscious mind.

Emotional Release: Individuals may experience emotional release and insights into past experiences.

## The Optimal Duration: How Long Should a Hypnotherapy Session Be?

Hypnotherapy sessions can last anywhere from 45 minutes to 2 hours, depending on individual needs and the complexity of the issues being addressed. Most initial sessions last around 60 to 90 minutes, allowing time for rapport-building and setting healing intentions. Subsequent sessions may vary in duration based on progress and therapeutic goals.

## The Inclusivity of Hypnosis: Can Everyone Be Hypnotized?

Contrary to common misconceptions, the ability to be hypnotized is not determined by one's strength of will or intelligence. In fact, most individuals can experience hypnosis to varying degrees. Hypnotic susceptibility varies from person to person, but nearly everyone can benefit from hypnotherapy to some extent. Skilled hypnotherapists tailor their approach to suit the unique needs and responses of each individual.

## Sample Hypnosis Script for Treating trauma, anxiety, fears, and negative emotions

As a certified clinical hypnotherapist, well-versed in the therapeutic power of hypnotherapy, I invite you to immerse yourself in the art of healing through Milton Erickson's Ericksonian naturalistic style of hypnosis. This full-length hypnosis script aims to address trauma, anxiety, fears, and negative emotions, guiding individuals on a transformative journey toward emotional liberation and serenity.

### Title: "Embracing Serenity: A Journey of Healing through Ericksonian Hypnosis"

[Begin by creating a relaxing atmosphere, using soft music or nature sounds, and encouraging the listener to find a comfortable position.]

## Introduction:

Welcome to this journey of healing and inner transformation. In the following moments, you will embark on a path of profound self-discovery and emotional liberation. As you allow yourself to relax, you will access the depths of your subconscious mind, unlocking the power to release trauma, anxiety, fears, and negative emotions. With each word and suggestion, you will find yourself feeling more empowered, calm, and centered.

## Induction:

Take a deep breath in, and as you exhale, close your eyes. Feel the weight of the world gently lifting off your shoulders. Relax your body and let go of any tension. Allow your mind to drift, like a leaf carried by a gentle breeze. As you continue to breathe deeply, imagine yourself standing in a peaceful forest, surrounded by the beauty of nature. The air is crisp, and the scent of earth and pine fills the air.

## Deepening:

With each breath you take, imagine yourself descending a staircase, one step at a time. As you descend, feel a sense of tranquility and comfort enveloping you. Each step takes you deeper into a state of profound relaxation. Ten... nine... eight... you feel safe and secure, seven... six... five... your mind becoming more receptive to positive change, four...

three... two... a serene stillness embracing you, one... you have reached the deepest level of relaxation.

## The Healing Garden:

Now, imagine yourself entering a beautiful healing garden within your mind. This garden represents your inner sanctuary—a place of healing and transformation. As you explore this garden, you notice a pool of clear, sparkling water. This pool symbolizes your emotional well-being and the purity of your essence.

## Releasing the Past:

Gently immerse your hands into the pool, feeling the healing water caressing your skin. As you do, imagine any traumas, anxieties, fears, and negative emotions being released from your being. See them transforming into ripples on the surface of the water, dissipating into the ether. Feel the weight of these burdens lifting from your heart, leaving you with a sense of lightness and freedom.

## The Power Within:

Within you lies an infinite reservoir of strength and resilience. Imagine this power as a warm, golden light emanating from your core. With each breath, this light expands, enveloping every part of your being. It flows through your veins, rejuvenating every cell in your body. You are a beacon of inner strength and serenity.

## Positive Affirmations:

Now, repeat these positive affirmations silently in your mind:

I am deserving of peace and healing.
I release all that no longer serves me.
I am strong and capable of overcoming challenges.
I embrace my emotions with love and compassion.
I am in control of my thoughts and feelings.

## Integration:

As you internalize these affirmations, imagine them being etched into the depths of your subconscious mind. Your mind is a fertile ground for positive transformation, and these affirmations will guide you toward emotional liberation and a renewed sense of self.

## Returning to Conscious Awareness:

[End the hypnosis session with gentle suggestions for reawakening, such as counting up from one to five, feeling more alert and refreshed with each number, and suggesting that the listener will carry this sense of serenity and empowerment into their daily life.]

Now, it is time to gently bring your awareness back to the present moment. You are fully in control, and whenever you are ready, you can open your eyes, feeling refreshed, revitalized, and centered.

**Conclusion:**

Remember, this journey of healing is within your reach whenever you need it. By revisiting this healing garden within your mind, you can continue to release trauma, anxiety, fears, and negative emotions, embracing serenity and emotional freedom. You hold the key to your own transformation, and as you nurture your inner sanctuary, you will find the calm within, guiding you toward a life of emotional balance and profound well-being.

This full-length hypnosis script harnesses the power of Milton Erickson's Ericksonian naturalistic style of hypnosis, guiding individuals on a journey of inner healing and emotional liberation. With each carefully crafted suggestion, this script empowers individuals to release trauma, anxiety, fears, and negative emotions, embracing serenity and profound transformation within themselves.

## Summary of Chapter 6:

Diving into Chapter 6 of "The Calm Within," readers are invited to explore the mysterious realm of hypnotherapy. This chapter's articles illuminate the profound potential of hypnotherapy in liberating individuals from the grip of trauma, anxiety, stress, and fear.

In clear and concise language, this chapter offers a guided tour of various hypnosis techniques—stage hypnosis, hypnotherapy, self-hypnosis, and natural hypnosis. The information helps to demystify the process, emphasizing the role of skilled therapists and the personalized duration of sessions.

With empathy and assurance, the chapter summaries underline the transformative journey that hypnotherapy can initiate. By unraveling the intricate interplay between the subconscious mind and emotional well-being, readers are empowered to envision a path toward emotional healing.

This chapter serves as a compass for individuals seeking emotional equilibrium. It showcases hypnotherapy as an avenue for rewriting one's emotional narrative, inspiring readers to embark on a profound expedition of self-discovery, resilience, and inner serenity.

*"The Butterfly's Flight"*

*In the flutter of a butterfly's flight,*
*Tranquility takes its gentle height.*
*On painted wings, it carries a plea,*
*Serenity's beauty, for all to see.*

# Universal Energy - Tap into the Healing Power of the Universe

"When you have found inner peace, you are in constant contact with the source of universal energy and cannot be tired. . . You have endless energy."

- Peace Pilgrim

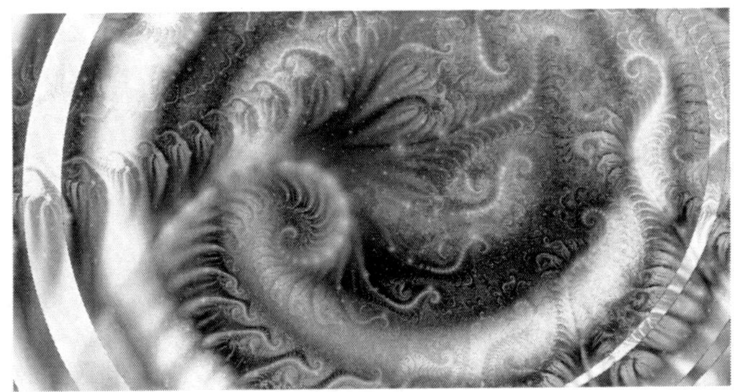

*Colors shift, clarity uplifts.*

In this enlightening chapter, we will explore the transformative nature of Universal Energy and its ability to bring harmony and balance to our being. By harnessing the energetic forces that permeate the universe, we can restore our inner vitality, align with our true essence, and experience profound healing at a soul level.

In the realm of holistic healing, Universal Energy Therapies have emerged as powerful tools for addressing trauma, anxiety, fears, and negative emotions. These therapies, such as Healing Touch, Therapeutic Touch, Reiki, and more, harness the subtle energies surrounding the body to promote emotional balance, inner peace, and overall well-being. As an expert on this subject, we delve into the transformative potential of Universal Energy Therapies and how they can empower individuals to find the calm within, releasing the burdens that weigh upon their hearts.

## Understanding the Energy Field:

At the core of Universal Energy Therapies lies the belief that the human body is surrounded by an energy field, often referred to as the aura. This field is interconnected with our physical, mental, emotional, and spiritual aspects, forming a dynamic and ever-changing tapestry of energy. When trauma, anxiety, fears, or negative emotions are experienced, these disturbances can manifest as imbalances or blockages in the energy field. Universal Energy Therapies seek to restore harmony within this field, enabling the natural flow of healing energy throughout the body.

## Techniques in Universal Energy Therapies:

Various techniques are employed within Universal Energy Therapies to facilitate healing and emotional release. Some of the common techniques include:

Chakra Clearing: Chakras are energy centers located along the body's midline. Practitioners work to balance and cleanse these chakras, removing energetic blockages and allowing for a harmonious flow of energy.

Mind Clearing: In this technique, the practitioner helps individuals release negative thought patterns and beliefs, promoting mental clarity and emotional well-being.

Laying on of Hands: Practitioners place their hands gently on or above specific areas of the body to channel healing energy, providing a soothing and calming effect.

Magnetic Unruffling: This technique involves using the hands to smooth and balance the energy field, encouraging the release of stagnant energy.

Aura Sweeping: Practitioners use their hands to sweep through the energy field, clearing away any disturbances and fostering a sense of renewal.

## The Experience of Universal Energy Therapy:

During a Universal Energy Therapy session, individuals often experience a deep sense of relaxation and peace. Some may feel warmth, tingling, or a gentle sensation as the healing energy flows through them. Emotional release is common, and individuals may find themselves shedding tears, feeling a weight lifted from their hearts. As the session progresses, a profound sense of connectedness and inner harmony may envelop the recipient.

## Session Length and Positive Benefits:

The duration of a Universal Energy Therapy session varies, but it typically lasts between 30 to 90 minutes. For best results, individuals may benefit from multiple sessions, depending on the complexity of their emotional challenges.

## The positive benefits of Universal Energy Therapy are vast:

Stress Reduction: Universal Energy Therapies are renowned for reducing stress and promoting relaxation. They help individuals unwind, allowing the body and mind to find equilibrium.

Emotional Liberation: By clearing energetic blockages and imbalances, Universal Energy Therapies aid in releasing trauma, anxiety, fears, and negative emotions, leading to emotional freedom and healing.

Enhanced Well-Being: Universal Energy Therapies stimulate the body's natural healing processes, supporting overall physical and emotional well-being.

Boosted Immunity: With the restoration of energy balance, the body's immune system is strengthened, promoting better health and resilience.

Increased Self-Awareness: Universal Energy Therapies encourage introspection and self-awareness, enabling individuals to gain insights into their emotional challenges and growth opportunities.

## Summary of Chapter 7:

Universal Energy Therapies offer individuals a profound path to embrace serenity, release trauma, anxiety, fears, and negative emotions, and connect with the calm within. By tapping into the healing power of the universe, individuals can unlock the potential for emotional liberation and transformation. The practice of Universal Energy Therapies serves as a gentle yet powerful support on the journey toward emotional healing and a life of profound well-being.

In this chapter, we explored the transformative realm of Universal Energy Therapies, unveiling how they can effectively address trauma, anxiety, fears, and negative emotions. Through techniques like Chakra Clearing, Mind Clearing, Laying on of Hands, Magnetic Unruffling, and Aura Sweeping, Universal Energy Therapies empower individuals to access their inner calm and achieve emotional liberation. With the power of the universe at their disposal, individuals can embark on a journey of healing and self-discovery, finding the serenity they seek amidst life's challenges.

*"The Whispers of Wind"*

*In the whispers of the gentlest wind,*
*Tranquility's secrets are gently pinned.*
*They murmur softly, a soothing sound,*
*Serenity found, in nature's surround.*

# Tips, Hints, and Techniques for Building Inner Harmony

"Getting over a painful event is much like crossing monkey bars. You have to let go at some point in order to move forward."

- C.S. Lewis

# The Power of Aromas: How Essential Oils Affect the Brain and Emotions

In the enchanting world of natural therapies, essential oils have captured the hearts of many seeking to find the calm within and overcome trauma, anxiety, stress, and fear. The captivating aromas from these oils can profoundly impact our emotions, bringing about a sense of serenity and emotional balance. In this section of this chapter, we explore how these aromatic wonders work with the brain and the limbic system, fostering emotional well-being and resilience.

## The Journey of Aromas:

When we inhale the captivating scents of essential oils, a fascinating journey begins. The olfactory glands in the nose play a crucial role in this process. As we breathe in the aroma, the olfactory receptors send signals to the limbic system, an intricate network of brain structures responsible for our emotions, memories, and behaviors.

## The Limbic System and Emotional Resilience:

The limbic system comprises several glands, each contributing to our emotional well-being and resilience.

Hypothalamus: This master gland regulates our autonomic nervous system and the release of hormones that govern our stress response, sleep, and appetite. When exposed to certain essential oils, the hypothalamus can trigger a relaxation response, promoting a sense of calmness and reducing stress.

Amygdala: The amygdala is associated with emotional processing and memory. Essential oil aromas can evoke memories and emotions linked to past experiences. By harnessing these aromas, individuals can address emotional wounds and traumas, fostering healing and resilience. The amygdala is responsible for processing positive emotions such as happiness, as well as negative ones, thus a person may be able to recover from trauma, anxiety, stress, and fear more easily with the appropriate use of supportive essential oils.

Hippocampus: This gland plays a vital role in memory consolidation and learning. The aroma of certain essential oils has been found to enhance memory retention and cognitive functions, supporting mental clarity during challenging times.

Thalamus: Responsible for sensory processing, the thalamus is activated by essential oil aromas, heightening sensory experiences and influencing emotional responses.

Pineal Gland: Often referred to as the "third eye," the pineal gland regulates circadian rhythms and sleep-wake cycles. The calming aromas of essential oils can promote better sleep, helping individuals rejuvenate and restore emotional balance.

Pituitary Gland: Known as the "master gland," the pituitary gland regulates the endocrine system and the release of hormones. Essential oil aromas can influence hormone secretion, leading to improved mood and emotional stability.

## The Emotion-Brain Connection:

Aromas from essential oils interact with the limbic system and its various glands, shaping our emotional experiences. When faced with adversity, these aromatic wonders can act as powerful allies, empowering individuals to navigate challenges with grace and resilience.

## Building Emotional Resilience:

By engaging the olfactory glands and the limbic system, essential oils offer a unique approach to emotional healing and resilience-building:

Emotional Release: Essential oils can unlock suppressed emotions, allowing individuals to process and release emotional burdens, fostering a sense of liberation and renewal.

Stress Reduction: Certain aromas can soothe the nervous system and reduce stress, providing a sanctuary of tranquility amidst life's pressures.

Emotional Grounding: The aromas of grounding essential oils can anchor individuals in the present moment, enhancing emotional stability and fortitude.

Encouraging Self-Reflection: As essential oils evoke memories and emotions, individuals can use this introspective space to gain insights and self-awareness, supporting personal growth and healing.

## Embrace the Power of Aromas:

Incorporating essential oils into daily life can be a powerful step towards finding the calm within and building emotional resilience. By understanding the intricate dance between aromas, the brain, and the limbic system, individuals can unlock the transformative potential of these aromatic wonders and embrace serenity on their journey of emotional healing.

In this section, we explored the enchanting world of aromas and their profound impact on emotions. By understanding how essential oils interact with the olfactory glands and the limbic system in the brain, individuals can harness the power of these aromatic wonders to build emotional resilience and overcome trauma, anxiety, stress, and fear. With the calming aromas of essential oils as their allies, individuals can embrace serenity and find the calm within amidst life's challenges.

## Extending The Power of Aromatherapy:

When inhaled or applied to the skin, essential oils can interact with the limbic system in the brain, an ancient part responsible for emotions, memories, and motivation.

## Coupling Aromatherapy with Intent:

The limbic system plays a vital role in linking scents with emotions and memories. When combined with specific intentions, the scent of a chosen essential oil can act as a powerful trigger throughout the day, gently reminding individuals of their goals and aspirations.

1. Setting Intentions: Setting clear intentions is the first step towards achieving a desired outcome. By establishing specific and positive goals, individuals can direct their focus and energy toward their aspirations.
2. Choosing the Right Essential Oil: Each essential oil possesses unique properties that can complement specific intentions. For example, lavender is known for promoting relaxation and stress relief, while peppermint is invigorating and energizing. By selecting an oil that aligns with the intended goal, individuals can enhance the effects of their intentions.
3. Application Methods: Applying a drop or two of the chosen essential oil to pulse points, such as wrists or temples, allows the aroma to be released throughout the day as body heat activates the scent. This continuous release of the aroma subconsciously reinforces the intended goal, creating a sense of focus and motivation.
4. Inhalation Techniques: Inhaling the aroma directly from the bottle or using a diffuser in the living or working space ensures that the scent is always present, gently nudging individuals to stay connected with their goals.

5. Mindful Practice: Throughout the day, individuals can take a moment to pause and inhale the scent consciously, reinforcing their intentions and realigning their focus.

## The Subconscious Guide:

The beauty of coupling aromatherapy with intent lies in its subtle yet profound impact on the subconscious mind. As the aroma of the essential oil is released, it acts as a gentle guide, nudging individuals back to their intentions and supporting them on their journey toward achieving their goals.

## Building Emotional Resilience:

By integrating the power of aromatherapy and intention, individuals can build emotional resilience and foster a calm and focused mindset. As the limbic system responds to the scent of the essential oil, positive emotions and memories associated with the intention are activated, creating a subconscious association between the aroma and the goal.

## Incorporating Aromatherapy into Daily Life:

Incorporating aromatherapy with intent into daily life can be a simple yet profound practice. Whether it's starting the morning with a few mindful inhales of an energizing essential oil or taking a moment during the day to reconnect with the chosen scent, this technique can serve as a gentle yet potent reminder of one's aspirations and guide them towards a sense of inner calm and achievement.

In this section, we explored the fascinating connection between aromatherapy, the limbic system, and setting intentions. By coupling the scent of a chosen essential oil with specific goals, individuals can harness the power of their subconscious mind to stay focused and motivated throughout the day. By incorporating this practice into daily life, readers can embrace the serenity within and work towards overcoming trauma, anxiety, stress, and fear, while building emotional resilience and achieving their desired goals.

## Exploring Essential Oils Yourself:

Congratulations on embarking on your journey toward holistic well-being and inner transformation! Throughout the first chapter of The Calm Within, you have explored the remarkable benefits of single essential oils and how they can enhance your physical, emotional, and spiritual health. In addition to single essential oils, blended essential oils are also used. Various single essential oils that complement each other can work synergistically together in an essential oil blend and will enhance the single essential oils for more effective therapies to help specific conditions that a person experiences.

High-quality essential oils, sourced online from reputable suppliers, play a pivotal role in this holistic approach. To ensure their purity and efficacy, these oils undergo rigorous Gas Chromatography-Mass Spectrometry (GC-MS) testing. GC-MS, a sophisticated analytical tool, dissects oils into their constituents, unveiling their chemical nature and ensuring their therapeutic integrity.

Among the spectrum of blends, transformative possibilities await those grappling with trauma, anxiety, fears, or negative emotions. Look for blends that address calming effects on many levels while still including invigorating essential oils, and blends that are formulated to offer holistic support, encouraging personal growth and emotional healing relative to the condition being experienced.

On the journey towards well-being, one doesn't need to stand alone. There are robust online communities, shared among millions worldwide, that advocate for the power of essential oils and holistic wellness. Through these connections, one gains access to exclusive resources, support, and educational opportunities that empower self-care and extend healing to others. Test the waters with caution and if you feel uncomfortable in a group, just move on to another one. Generally, people in essential oils communities are friendly and supportive, but some groups have strong feelings about their methods of applying essential oils and/or about their favorite brands of essential oils. Using essential oils is partly science, partly art, and partly intuition so explore the world with an open mind and enjoy the experiences you encounter along the way.

It's important to underscore that safety and proper usage are paramount when navigating the world of essential oils. Comprehensive educational materials, including workshops, webinars, and guides, are readily available to ensure informed and confident use.

Is it time to embark on this empowering path with high-quality essential oils? Begin your journey by selecting a reputable source of high-quality essential oils, obtaining books, and researching which oils would best suit your needs. Your adventure towards holistic wellness is uniquely yours, and the exploration of essential oils is a transformative step towards nurturing both the mind and the soul.

## My Passion with Essential Oils

My journey began one weekend while we were enjoying a day browsing through New Age stores in Victoria to find new crystals and books on natural healing therapies. We came across a display of essential oils and test-smelled some. I bought a few dram-size (4.5ml) bottles and took them home. Since I didn't have any experience with essential oils, I just applied them like I had seen other people put on colognes and perfumes. I never noticed any effects at the time and just enjoyed the smells.

The next morning, I woke up with a terrific headache but didn't associate it with the essential oils I had applied the day before. After my morning shower, I noticed the headache had reduced. I realized that the essential oils might have had something to do with the headache, so I did some online research and found out that some essential oils can cause adverse reactions if they are adulterated or poor quality. The oils I had bought only had a handwritten label with only the names of the essential oils on them. There was no manufacturer's name or other information on the labels, not even the store name.

The limited research I had done intrigued my curiosity and I continued to research more about essential oils on the internet. I came across an ad for a free research report that had been done by a reputable source and a free sample of an essential oil from a company that tested all the essential oils they sold.

A couple weeks later I received a large envelope in the mail which contained the free research report and a sandwich-size baggie with a cotton ball in it with a drop of an essential oil blend called Joy. There were instructions in the package on how I could buy high-quality essential oils from this company called Young Living Essential Oils. It turned out to be a referral network system, and I could earn a small commission on the purchases by those people who I referred to Young Living Essential Oils.

The smell of the Joy essential oil blend was heavenly, and I was really excited about sharing this with friends, so I signed up right away, and made my first order for an "Essential 7" package of essential oils. Then, I took my baggie with the drop of Joy on the cotton ball around to several friends, to take a whiff. The reaction was the same as when I first smelled the "Joy" and before I even received my "Essential 7" package, I had referred enough people to Young Living

Essential Oils, that I reached "Executive" level in the Young Living system, and I started receiving referral payments right away. That was 26 years ago, and I have been receiving referral payments from Young Living Essential Oils since July 1997. I still have my original "Essential 7" package with the original bottle of Joy still in it.

Young Living Essential Oils is a leader in the field of essential oils and now has decades of experience in distilling, producing, and blending the finest oils available on the market today. Young Living set the standard for essential oils and essential oil products, starting in 1993. Young Living Essential Oils are tested multiple times before being bottled. These tests include Gas Chromatography and Mass Spectrometry. A gas chromatography-mass spectrometry (GC-MS) equipment enables technicians to separate a sample into its individual parts and analyze each for its chemical properties.

Young Living is an online marketing company that now has over 6 million members worldwide. Anyone can join Young Living, either as a Customer or as a Brand Partner through a referral link and gain access to a supportive community of like-minded individuals who are passionate about holistic wellness and the power of essential oils. Both Customers and Brand Partners receive exclusive perks and educational resources. In addition, Brand Partners purchase Young Living products at wholesale prices and earn rewards through Young Living's generous loyalty program.

Remember, when using essential oils, it is essential to prioritize safety and proper usage. Young Living provides comprehensive educational materials, including workshops, webinars, and informative guides, to support you in using essential oils effectively and confidently. To become a valued member of Young Living Essential Oils, you can use the QR Code or click the image with the QR Code below to start your journey with Young Living Essential Oils. You can also call Young Living Essential Oils at their Global Headquarters at 1-801-418-8900 and speak to Customer Service in order to become a member. You can mention that you were referred to by Brooks Allisen or Allisen Consulting Ltd., Brand Partner #100221.

## One Word That Makes a Difference in Your Progress

The word is "can".

How does the word "can" make a difference in your progress in overcoming trauma, anxiety, stress, fears, and/or negative emotions?

Your brain is pretty smart and understands specific language very well. When it hears the word "can" in a sentence, such as "I can do…", it searches through the list of things that it knows your body and/or your mind is capable of doing and when it determines that you are capable of doing the task, it is satisfied that you are capable of doing the task. This doesn't mean that it understands that your goal is to do the task, it just acknowledges that you are capable of performing the task.

Say that you want to accomplish something significant in your life and you decide on a specific goal. You keep telling yourself that you can accomplish this goal. Your mind understands your words and agrees that you can accomplish the goal, however, that's as far as it goes. Your mind isn't on track to help you accomplish your goal.

By altering your words slightly, your mind will be working to help you reach your goal.

Do you want to try a little experiment, using a coin, to see how this actually works?

Hold a coin between your index finger and your thumb. Stretch your arm out in front of you horizontally, still holding the coin between your index finger and your thumb, keeping your other fingers back and out of the way. Focus on the coin as hard as you are able to, and when you are ready, THINK these words and say them to yourself - don't say the words out loud, just focus on THINKING these words and saying them silently to yourself "I can drop it, I can drop it, I can drop it". While repeating those words to yourself over and over again - and while thinking and saying the words to yourself, try to open your finger and thumb. It is impossible. Your brain is saying Okay, okay, I'm standing by, I'm standing by - waiting for the command to drop the coin. You haven't given your brain or your biocomputer any instructions to complete a task. You need to activate the mechanism that releases the coin.

Delete the word "can" and repeat the process. This time change the words you are thinking and the words you are saying to yourself to: "I drop it" or to "Drop it", and see what happens.

In order to achieve what was set out to accomplish we must use words that activate our goal-achieving mechanism, and eliminate those words that sideline us or leave us wondering why we aren't getting where we want to be.

## The Brain Understands Positive Instructions

In the fascinating realm of healing trauma, anxiety, stress, and fear, the use of positively worded commands or instructions holds a special place. Understanding how the brain processes language sheds light on why positively phrased commands are more effective than negatively worded ones.

The Brain's Language Processing:

The brain is a marvelous organ with a complex system for processing language. When we hear or read words, our brain immediately goes to work, deciphering the meaning behind the language. However, the brain has an interesting quirk—it does not process negatively phrased commands or instructions in the same way it processes positive ones.

## Why Negatively Worded Commands Don't Work:

The brain has difficulty processing negatively phrased commands or instructions that contain words like "not" or "n't." For instance, if someone says, "Don't think of a pink elephant," your brain's automatic response is to conjure up an image of a pink elephant before attempting not to think about it. It's almost as if the brain misses the "don't" part and focuses on the subject of the command.

## The Power of Positively Worded Commands:

On the other hand, positively phrased commands or instructions directly convey what we want to achieve, providing the brain with a clear direction. When we say, "Think of a white dove," the brain effortlessly creates an image of a white dove, following the instructions precisely.

## Harnessing the Brain's Response:

Understanding how the brain processes language allows us to harness this response in various therapeutic techniques, such as hypnotherapy or positive affirmations.

Hypnotherapy: Skilled hypnotherapists utilize the power of positive phrasing to guide individuals into a state of deep relaxation and receptivity to positive suggestions. By framing suggestions positively, the brain readily accepts and internalizes these affirmations, leading to positive changes in thoughts, behaviors, and emotions.

Positive Affirmations: Practicing positive affirmations involves repeating empowering statements in the present tense. When positively phrased, such as "I am confident and capable," these affirmations create a profound impact on the subconscious mind, nurturing self-belief and resilience.

Self-Talk: Becoming aware of one's self-talk and transforming negative statements into positive ones can lead to significant shifts in mindset and emotional well-being. Instead of saying, "I can't handle this," try saying, "I am capable of handling challenges."

## Embrace the Power of Positivity:

In the journey of healing and embracing serenity, utilizing the power of positively worded commands can be a transformative tool. By understanding how the brain responds to language, individuals can tap into the innate ability to foster positive changes within themselves, enhancing emotional well-being and overcoming adversity.

In this section, we looked into the fascinating way the brain processes language, particularly how it responds to positively worded commands versus negatively phrased ones. Understanding this distinction allows individuals to harness the brain's natural inclination towards positive phrasing in therapeutic techniques like hypnotherapy and affirmations.

By embracing the power of positivity, individuals can cultivate a deeper sense of calm, overcome trauma, anxiety, stress, and fear, and step into a realm of emotional healing and resilience.

## Learn How To Muscle Test Yourself

The author mentions muscle testing several times in "The Calm Within". Maybe you know what that means? Maybe you would like to know more about muscle testing? Maybe be able to do it for yourself? Maybe you would like to get some answers about your body or what might or might not be good for your body or your mind? Maybe you would like to access your subconscious mind and find out what it is thinking? Maybe you would like some help making decisions on things that you don't fully understand or have all the information on - things your subconscious mind has access to that your conscious mind is not fully aware of? Or maybe you would like to connect through Universal Energy to realms you have dreamed of, but never knew you could access? If those ideas intrigue you, learning how to muscle test might be beneficial in your journey in this life.

In simple terms, muscle testing is receiving a physical response from your subconscious mind via the muscles that the subconscious mind can cause reactions that can be seen or felt. These muscle movements are referred to as ideomotor responses and are involuntary muscle movements triggered by the subconscious brain.

The subconscious mind is responsible for all autonomic functions in the body, so it understands the body better than the conscious mind, hence when you are muscle testing, you are getting answers about the body directly from the central biocomputer that is running the body's biological functions. You are talking to the master coordinator of the whole body's physical systems, so to speak. The subconscious mind also has access to the brain's memory banks and can retrieve information about the body that a person doesn't recall or maybe even know is there. The subconscious mind is also a whiz at calculations and analysis, so it can be very helpful in answering questions that the conscious mind is not able to. It's a person's built-in artificial intelligence program that is running 24/7/365, and it's there to use to help you move forward in life.

As a person starts on the path of doing muscle testing, one of the easiest ways to see the connection working is to use a pendulum. A pendulum does not have to be elaborate or sophisticated. A lightweight string or chain and a weighted object, like a metal washer or a house key will do. The string or chain does not need to be longer than 4-5 inches or 10-12 cm.

Below is a circle with a cross in it and the words "Yes" at the top and bottom of the vertical part of the cross, and "No" at either end of the horizontal part of the cross. The initial objective is to hold the weight of the pendulum above the point where the two lines cross. Sitting at a table or desk, hold your arm out so the pendulum dangles over the center of the cross. Do not rest your elbow on the table, the arm of the chair, or any part of your body. Your arm should be bent at the elbow and be able to move freely.

Suspend the weight just above the cross, just so it doesn't touch the cross. DO NOT MOVE YOUR HAND. Look at the weight, and without taking your eyes off the weight, IMAG-INE that the weight is moving forwards, backward, forwards, backward: Yes - Yes, Yes - Yes, Yes - Yes. Consistently and continuously repeat the words to yourself and imagine the direction of the pendulum. Expect to see just a little move-ment in the pendulum, in the direction you are imagining it to be moving. Follow the same process in the side-to-side direction - right, left, right, left: No – No, No - No, No - No. When you want the weight on the pendulum to stop moving, use your imagination to think about something unrelated to the cross and the pendulum, and watch it stop swinging.

Once you have successfully practiced with the pendulum in both directions, you can start asking simple yes and no ques-tions with known answers, like "Does salt taste like horse-radish?" or "Can I constantly hold my breath for a full 10 minutes?" or "Is the moon made of cheese?" or "Are twelve eggs the same as a dozen eggs?" or "Are elephants larger than dog fleas?", etc. You can also say the words "Give me a Yes" or "Give me a No", to test that your muscle testing skills are turned on, before you start to ask your questions.

Once you are satisfied with the consistency of getting yes or no answers to known questions, you can start experimenting with your questions, then when you are sure you are getting consistently correct answers, you can start checking whether or not things you are not sure about are good for you or not. Your subconscious mind knows the correct answer, so you are beginning to connect to your subconscious mind for the answers you want to know. You can never have too much practice using your pendulum to get the answers to your questions.

As you become more adept and confident in using a pendulum to muscle test, you can start testing for such things as: which essential oil(s) would benefit me the most, or which supplement(s) would support my body and/or mind the best. You can even hold a bottle of essential oil in your hand and ask about its quality and whether or not it contains adulterated, synthetic, or inferior components.

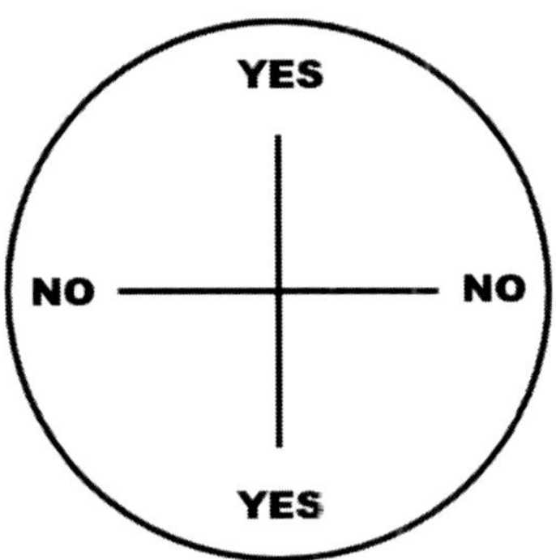


*"Yes" – "No" Basic Muscle Testing Chart*

In addition to your "Yes" and "No" muscle testing, you can phrase questions so that you get more detail, such as "Is there a 50% (...60%, 70%, etc.) or higher percentage benefit in (this product or service) for me"? Or you can muscle test to ask your body, "How many (things) is the most beneficial number (test for "Yes" or "No" for 1, 2, 3, etc.) of (things) for me to use at this time"? You can also test anything you can think of, just by phrasing your question so that the answer will be either a "Yes" or a "No".

Further to practicing using your pendulum, there are several other techniques you can use to get answers from your subconscious mind. For example, there is the body pendulum, where you feel a slight movement forward with your body when the answer is yes, and a slight movement backward for a no. Another technique is to use your fingers. Make a circle with your index finger and the thumb of your left hand. Make a similar circle with your right hand, except make the right-hand circle intertwine with the left-hand circle. Try to pull one through the other. If you are successful, that indicates a "yes", if the circles lock up and you can't pull through, that is a "no". This technique takes some practice, but when you get it, you can be anywhere and ask your subconscious a question and get an answer. Several other techniques are even more inconspicuous, but they are a little more advanced for this session.

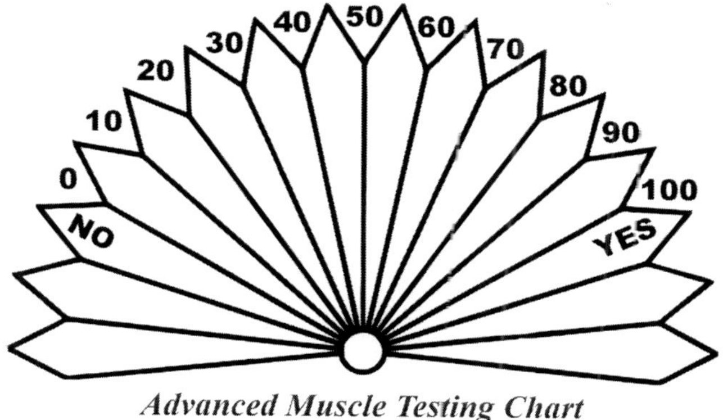



*Advanced Muscle Testing Chart*

Once you are proficient with the basic Yes-Yes, No-No cross chart, you can get more detailed answers with a fan chart, such as the one above. The numbers 0 to 100 can be percentages instead of a simple "Yes" or "No". 0 can be your "No" and 100 can be your "Yes". In other words, when you practice with the fan muscle testing chart, you can tell your subconscious mind that the number "0" is the same as "No" on the cross-circle basic muscle testing chart and that the number "100" is the same as "Yes" on the cross-circle chart. When you use the fan muscle testing chart, you can substitute the numbers. For instance, each number can be reduced by a factor of 10, thus 20 becomes 2, 50 becomes 5, 80 becomes 8, and 100 becomes 10. Now you can find out which item in a list of less than 10 items is the first or best choice, second choice, etc. There is no end to the number of questions the fan chart can give you answers to. Remember to keep practicing and finding answers to things you thought you would never find - and have fun.

## Embracing a Positive Self-Image for Transformation

In the journey of releasing trauma, anxiety, stress, fears, and negative emotions, one often encounters the profound impact of self-image. A healthy and positive self-image can act as a catalyst, transforming a person from being negatively affected by their past experiences to embracing a brighter and more fulfilling future. Let's explore the importance of self-image and its effects on personal transformation.

Embracing Self-Compassion: Acknowledging that past experiences do not define one's worth is a pivotal step toward building a positive self-image. Practicing self-compassion allows a person to release self-judgment and criticism, making room for self-acceptance and growth.

Releasing Limiting Beliefs: Recognize and release limiting beliefs that hinder personal growth. By identifying and reframing these beliefs, a person can shift their perspectives and embrace a more empowering narrative about themselves and their capabilities.

Cultivating a Growth Mindset: Focusing on a growth mindset enables a person to view challenges as opportunities for learning and development. Embracing the idea that one's abilities can be developed through dedication and hard work fosters resilience and a positive outlook on life.

Setting Positive Intentions: Visioning a positive self-image and setting clear intentions for personal growth can create a roadmap for transformation. By visualizing oneself as confident, capable, and resilient, individuals can begin to embody these qualities in their daily lives.

Tapping into Inner Strength: Learning to tap into inner strength and harness it to overcome adversity is a concept that empowers a person to navigate challenging situations with confidence and grace. Recognizing the resilience that lies within oneself fosters a sense of empowerment.

Seeking Supportive Communities: By surrounding themselves with supportive communities and mentors provides a person with a nurturing environment for personal growth. Connecting with like-minded individuals who share similar aspirations can offer valuable encouragement and validation.

Celebrating Progress: Recognizing and celebrating small wins and achievements along the way reinforces a positive self-image. By acknowledging progress, individuals can build a sense of accomplishment and momentum toward greater transformation.

## The Ripple Effect of Positive Self-Image:

Transforming one's self-image from negative to positive sets in motion a powerful ripple effect that impacts various aspects of life. As a person begins to view themselves with love, respect, and confidence, their attitudes toward challenges, relationships, and opportunities shift.

Increased Resilience: A positive self-image strengthens emotional resilience, enabling individuals to bounce back from setbacks and challenges with a sense of determination.

Improved Confidence: Embracing a positive self-image instills a sense of self-assurance and belief in one's abilities, fostering a willingness to take on new opportunities.

Healthy Relationships: A positive self-image sets the foundation for healthy relationships, as individuals learn to value and respect themselves, thus attracting more positive and fulfilling connections with others.

Goal Achievement: Empowered by a positive self-image, individuals become more driven to pursue their aspirations, leading to greater success in various areas of life.

Emotional Well-Being: Cultivating a positive self-image positively impacts emotional well-being, reducing the impact of trauma, anxiety, stress, and negative emotions on daily life.

In this section, we explored the significance of cultivating a positive self-image as a transformative tool. Incorporating the teachings and approaches of prominent authors, presenters, coaches, counselors, teachers, and motivational speakers, a person is able to overcome adversity and embrace the calm within. Through self-compassion, releasing limiting beliefs, and adopting a growth mindset, a person will build a powerful foundation for personal growth and emotional well-being, unlocking the doors to a brighter future.

## Harnessing the Power of Positive Thought: Breaking Free from Looping Thoughts

In the labyrinth of the mind, looping thoughts can often entangle us, holding us back from progress and serenity. "The Calm Within" unveils a transformative technique to cut these mental knots and pave a path to positive thinking.

Here is a simple strategy to use to silence the clamor of looping thoughts. One says these words to themself "cancel, cancel, cancel - clear, clear, clear - next, next, next." This is repeated 3 times. This disrupts the cycle of unproductive thoughts. This three-step incantation acts as a mental reset button, offering liberation from the clutches of negativity.

" Cancel" stops the looping thought. "Clear" removes the looping thought. "Next" tells the mind to find the next thought to focus on. Repeating the phrase 3 times sends 9 words to the subconscious mind three times, which prepares it to accept new input.

The journey doesn't end there. To get an extra boost, a person can use the phrase "move on." This catalyst propels a person forward, ensuring that they transcend lingering thoughts and seize the reins of their thinking patterns.

In preparation for using these phrases, it is helpful to store uplifting memories and images - events, places, and people that stir joy. These golden memories act as bridges, gently transitioning the mind from looping thoughts to the vibrant tapestry of positivity.

"The Calm Within" empowers readers to rewrite the script of their inner dialogue. By embracing these techniques, a person can take control of their mental landscape, steering it towards what truly matters - progress, serenity, and self-discovery.

## Coloring Your Way to Serenity

In the heart of "The Calm Within," a unique path to healing awaits that combines creativity and tranquility - adult coloring. Diving into uncharted territories of emotional well-being, another avenue to healing opens up a vibrant picture of how the simple act of coloring can be an effective antidote for trauma, anxiety, stress, fears, and negative emotions. Adult coloring, often seen as a nostalgic pastime, has emerged as a powerful tool for self-expression and emotional release. There is a fascinating science behind this trend, highlighting how engaging in coloring ignites the brain's reward centers and triggers a meditative state. By focusing on intricate designs and coordinating colors, individuals effortlessly redirect their attention away from life's pressures. But it's not just about coloring within the lines; it's about coloring your world with positive emotions.

Discover the psychological magic of colors, and how specific shades can evoke various feelings. From soothing blues to vibrant yellows, readers explore a palette of emotions at their fingertips. While embracing creativity, individuals also cultivate mindfulness - a proven technique for managing emotional challenges, artfully intertwining practicality, and inspiring thoughts for participants to embark on their coloring journeys armed with newfound enthusiasm. Readers are encouraged to grasp coloring's therapeutic wand, transforming it into a powerful instrument for emotional well-being. Through every stroke of color, every shade chosen, and every intricate pattern, individuals discover not just artistic expression, but a refuge where trauma, anxiety, stress, fears, and negativity dissolve into the mesmerizing symphony of colors - a symphony that leads to serenity.

The following images may give you an idea of what you can expect to see in a coloring book designed for adults. There are many more coloring book genres to choose from. They come in the form of printed books or in the form of printables that you print on your own printer at home. There are millions of people engaging in coloring these days. It's become a huge opportunity for many people to relax and enjoy the peace of focusing on their creativity and engaging their imagination for hours at a time. Coloring is soothing to the mind and brings joy to the soul.

## *Sample Coloring Pages*

The above coloring pages are samples of botanical and flowers; a hobbit cottage in the woods; fantasy architecture in the future; and a stained-glass window from the 1930's.

## Summary of Chapter 8:

Within the pages of "The Calm Within," Chapter 8 emerges as a beacon of hope, guiding readers toward a profound connection with the universe's healing energy. The author's deft touch navigates the realm of Universal Energy Therapies, illuminating the transformative potential of modalities such as Healing Touch, Therapeutic Touch, Reiki, and more.

In this enlightening chapter, the reader is invited to explore the energy field that envelops us—the aura—and the incredible techniques that harness its power. With a blend of gentle guidance and expert insights, the author paints a vivid picture of Chakra Clearing, Mind Clearing, Laying on of Hands, Magnetic Unruffling, and Aura Sweeping, among other techniques.

This chapter not only demystifies Universal Energy Therapies but also accentuates their practicality. The reader is guided through sessions, their potential emotional journey, and the lasting benefits of these therapies. With empathy and clarity, the author instills confidence in readers, allowing them to tap into the boundless reservoir of universal energy for healing, strength, and emotional well-being.

Within the labyrinth of the mind, looping thoughts can ensnare, impeding progress and tranquility. In "The Calm Within," a transformative approach is revealed, offering liberation from this mental tangle. By saying "cancel, cancel, cancel - clear, clear, clear - next, next, next" three times, the grip of unproductive thoughts is disrupted. "Cancel" halts the loop, "clear" erases it, and "next" steers the mind toward new thoughts. Repeating this nine-word phrase thrice prepares the subconscious for renewal. To supercharge the technique, add "move on." This propels forward momentum, ensuring escape from lingering thoughts. Uplifting memories act as bridges, easing the transition from loops to positive vistas. This strategy empowers inner dialogue transformation, guiding minds towards progress, serenity, and self-discovery.

At the heart of "The Calm Within" lies a path of healing that melds creativity and tranquility—adult coloring. Beyond nostalgia, this activity proves a potent tonic for trauma, anxiety, stress, and negativity. Delve into the psychology of colors, discovering their emotional magic. From calming blues to vibrant yellows, readers can explore a spectrum of feelings with each stroke. Dive into the world of coloring's therapeutic wand, transforming it into an instrument for emotional well-being. It's not just coloring; it's painting your world with positivity. By wielding colors, readers sculpt a refuge where emotional burdens dissolve into the symphony of hues—an invitation to serenity. These techniques in coloring can provide solace for the mind and a canvas for the soul, offering relaxation and igniting creativity in a million shades of expression.

# 9

# Summary: Embracing the Calm Within

"The only journey is the one within."

- Rainer Maria Rilke

In the journey of releasing trauma, anxiety, stress, fears, and negative emotions, the quest for inner serenity takes center stage. The book "The Calm Within" explores a treasure trove of natural therapies that have the power to transform lives and restore emotional well-being. From Essential Oils and Spiritual Response Therapy to Biomagnetic Pair Therapy, Natural Supplements, Meditation, and Hypnotherapy, each modality serves as a powerful tool to unlock the path toward healing and growth.

## The Power of Natural Therapies:

### Essential Oils Soothe the Psyche

Through the guidance of this book, readers have discovered the profound effects of essential oils on the brain and emotions. From lavender's calming properties to peppermint's invigorating essence, these natural wonders have the potential to uplift moods and soothe frazzled nerves.

### Spiritual Response Therapy Calms the Past

Spiritual response therapy has illuminated the path toward releasing karmic patterns and embracing a future free from emotional burdens. By tapping into the depths of the subconscious mind, individuals can rewrite their life narratives and embrace newfound clarity and purpose.

## Restore Balance to the Internal Environment with Bio-magnetic Pair Therapy

The marvels of Biomagnetic Pair Therapy have allowed readers to restore electromagnetic balance which creates an environment that inhibits and restores function and pathogens, freeing themselves from the shackles of past traumas. With magnetic pairs guiding the body toward balance and harmony, emotional healing becomes an attainable reality.

## Fortifying with Natural Supplements:

The book has also revealed the wonders of natural supplements in building healthy neurological pathways. From herbs and vitamins to minerals and amino acids, these nourishing elements have empowered readers to support their emotional well-being and strengthen their resilience.

## Meditation and Hypnotherapy: The Gateway to Inner Peace:

Meditation and hypnotherapy have emerged as vital allies in the pursuit of emotional tranquility. By immersing in mindful practices and guided hypnosis, readers have discovered how to calm their nerves, restore focus, and reset their feelings of happiness.

**Harnessing Universal Energy:**

The book's exploration of universal energy therapies, such as Healing Touch, Therapeutic Touch, and Reiki, has offered readers a profound connection to the healing power of the universe. From the aura's energy field to Chakra Clearing and Mind Clearing, these therapies have opened the door to emotional healing and spiritual growth.

**Embracing a Positive Self-Image:**

The book's bonus chapter illuminated the significance of self-image in transforming one's life. By adopting a growth mindset, practicing self-compassion, and setting positive intentions, readers have discovered the gateway to personal empowerment and future success.

## A Roadmap to the Future:

As readers journey toward healing and emotional well-being, they must remember that transformation is a process. Each step taken, each moment of self-reflection, and each practice embraced contribute to the overall journey toward the calm within.

## Guidance for the Future:

For those experiencing trauma, anxiety, stress, fears, and negative emotions, the road ahead may seem daunting. Yet, armed with the wisdom of "The Calm Within," they possess a powerful toolkit to reclaim their peace.

Embrace Your Journey: Healing takes time, and each step forward is a victory. Embrace the process, acknowledging that growth comes with its share of challenges and triumphs.

Be Kind to Yourself: Practice self-compassion as you navigate through your emotions. Remember that healing is not linear, and it's okay to have ups and downs along the way.

Harness the Power of Natural Therapies: Continue exploring the natural therapies that resonate with you the most. Whether it's essential oils, meditation, or universal energy therapies, find what brings you inner peace and make it a part of your daily routine.

Seek Support and Guidance: Don't hesitate to reach out to professionals or supportive communities that can guide you in your healing journey.

Cultivate a Positive Self-Image: Celebrate your progress and envision a positive self-image. Believe in your potential and hold onto the vision of a brighter and calmer future.

As you embark on the path of healing, know that the essence of "The Calm Within" lies within you. Embrace these natural therapies, practice self-compassion, and cultivate a positive self-image, and you'll discover the strength to overcome trauma, anxiety, stress, fears, and negative emotions, transforming into a more resilient, serene, and empowered version of yourself. Remember, you are the author of your own story, and with each turn of the page, you create a future filled with peace, joy, and emotional well-being.

## May the journey towards the calm within be transformative and empowering.

In this concluding chapter, the reader is reminded of the transformative potential found within the pages of "The Calm Within." Embracing the power of natural therapies, the significance of a positive self-image, and the support of universal energy, readers are encouraged to continue their journey with patience and compassion. Armed with newfound knowledge and understanding, we are guided toward a future of emotional resilience and inner peace.

*"The Rain's Soft Embrace"*

*Raindrops fall with gentle grace,*
*Tranquility in their cool embrace.*
*As they cleanse the earth anew,*
*Serenity's gift, like morning dew.*

*Embrace the journey; success is your destination!*

# 10

# Continuing the Journey: Embracing The Future

"Your present circumstances don't determine where you can go; they merely determine where you start."

Nido Qubein

Having navigated the intricate tapestry of healing and self-discovery through the pages of The Calm Within, we stand at the threshold of a future adorned with serenity. The journey is not a mere recounting of insights; it's an invitation to carry the transformative wisdom into the uncharted territory that lies ahead.

In the wake of the book's guidance, prior setbacks may have come and gone, but they've become stepping stones, propelling us forward. The goal remains—a life adorned with peaceful serenity where negative emotions hold no sway.

The embracing power of Essential Oils, not just as scents but as companions, guides us toward a future where fragrant essences become a source of solace and strength.

Spiritual Response Therapy, once a chapter, is consistently helping us navigate and liberate ourselves from the echoes of the past.

*"Uncharted Victory"*

*In the labyrinth of challenges, uncharted,*
*Triumph emerges, adversity departed.*
*A bold horizon, dreams set free,*
*Triumph's embrace, our jubilee.*

Natural Supplements have evolved beyond interventions; they are now integrated into our routine, harmoniously nourishing both body and soul.

Meditation, once a sporadic event, is now a trusted practice, offering regular moments of meditative respite and access to the vast potential of our subconscious mind.

As we look toward the future, The Calm Within becomes not just a source of inspiration but a roadmap for implementing acquired wisdom in our daily lives.

The alchemy of these therapies intertwines seamlessly with our stories, empowering you to reclaim control over your emotional landscape.

Picture the future as a radiant beacon on the horizon, guiding us through challenges. The book is not a conclusion; it's a beginning—a continuous journey toward a future where anxiety, fears, and negative emotions gradually dissipate, making way for the perpetual dawn of serenity.

As we embrace the path that lies ahead, we acknowledge that this book is just a stepping stone in our ongoing journey. It is a continuous dance towards the tranquility we have envisioned. Standing on the edge of the unknown, let us allow the lessons we have learned to serve as the gentle breeze beneath our wings, propelling us towards a future abundant with peace and boundless opportunities.

*Life's turns lead to triumph, follow your path.*